THE C* WORD

(Confidence)

THE C* WORD

(Confidence)

MEL SCHILLING

murdoch books

Sydney | London

Published in 2022 by Murdoch Books, an imprint of Allen & Unwin

Murdoch Books Australia
83 Alexander Street, Crows Nest NSW 2065
Phone: +61 (0)2 8425 0100
murdochbooks.com.au
info@murdochbooks.com.au

Murdoch Books UK
Ormond House, 26–27 Boswell Street, London WC1N 3JZ
Phone: +44 (0) 20 8785 5995
murdochbooks.co.uk
info@murdochbooks.co.uk

 A catalogue record for this
book is available from the
National Library of Australia

A catalogue record for this book is available from the British Library

ISBN 9 781 92235 142 5 Australia
ISBN 9 781 91166 852 7 UK

Cover design by Emily O'Neill
Text design by Madeleine Kane
Cover photography by Zahrina Photography

Typeset by Midland Typesetters
Printed and bound by CPI Group (UK) Ltd, Croydon, CR04YY

10 9 8 7 6 5 4 3 2

CONTENTS

Introduction   1

PART 1: FEAR MASTERY   12
1   Fear is not your frenemy (even though it feels like she's
        ripping your heart out)   15
2   Be the boss of your imposter   39
3   Through their eyes   61

PART 2: SMART COURAGE   80
4   Smart Courage: The thinking woman's suit of armour   83
5   Time to put on your Big Girl Pants
        (with an extra-comfortable gusset)   101
6   From nice girl to courageous woman   129

PART 3: DEEP CONFIDENCE   150
7   Yes . . . you can   153
8   Two ways to build confidence
        (spoiler alert: only one truly works)   171
9   Bouncing back from a crisis of confidence   195

PART 4: FLUID COMPETENCE   218
10 Your success sweet spot   221
11 I should be so lucky!   241
12 Giving head to get ahead (not a chapter about porn)   259

Conclusion   279
Endnotes   284
Acknowledgments   287
About the author   288

I dedicate this book to my parents, Beth and Paul Schilling.

Mum, you taught me the definition of courage and overcoming fear. As a kid, I watched you face and overcome your fear of flying and then go on to travel the world. You showed me that fear can be temporary and can be overcome.

Dad, you showed me how to communicate with confidence. I watched you take command of countless dinner parties and barbecues, captivating people with your stories and inspiring others with your infectious energy. 'Good onya kid!'

INTRODUCTION

I'm so pleased you're here. Actually, I'm delighted.

There's a reason you picked up this book. Maybe the cheeky title appealed to you, perhaps you've seen me speaking on stage or it could be that you've seen me on the telly.

Or perhaps there's a deeper reason.

A reason that has nothing to do with me and everything to do with you. This book may have appealed to that little voice inside you that whispers 'you could be more confident'.

It might be that you find yourself gazing at more confident women with envious eyes, wondering what they have that you don't. Maybe you were once a more confident woman but something changed in your life and robbed you of that feeling. Or it could be that you feel confident in some areas of your life, but not others.

Perhaps you have a confidence gap.

Well, I'm here to tell you that you're in the right place – and you're not alone.

Most women I speak to tell me that they would love to have more confidence. They often share stories about the things in their lives that hold them back, the reasons why they can't do what they want to do or be who they want to be, and the external forces that stop them from living the lives they truly deserve. Some might call these 'excuses'.

I find one of the things that helps women to move past their excuses and start to step into their power is figuring out their WHY – that is, their deeper reason for wanting to be more confident. Sure, we all have some superficial reasons for wanting to be more confident:

- I could wear those skin-tight Kardashian-style jeans.
- My social media following would skyrocket.
- Everyone would admire me.
- I'd be a devil in the sack.

But when we dig beneath the surface, most women have strong, compelling, *meaningful* reasons for wanting to live a more confident life. I recently surveyed the women in my online community and, when asked what they would do if they had more confidence, they responded:

- start my own business
- quit my job
- let my walls down
- wear whatever I want
- enjoy parenting more
- have healthy relationships
- put myself out there in dating
- put myself out there in my career
- try new things
- progress in my career
- stand up for myself
- make better decisions
- be braver with public speaking
- share more ideas at work
- not allow others to mistreat me
- speak my truth
- believe in my worth
- help others be more confident.

Ultimately, I find that most women want to build their confidence so they can have a bigger positive impact on their own lives, on the people around them and on the planet at large.

It's about how you want to be remembered.

HOW TO MAKE A MEANINGFUL IMPACT THROUGH CONFIDENCE AND COURAGE

We all want to make a meaningful impact on the world.

We want to leave a legacy, to take comfort in the fact that we can go to sleep at night knowing we have made a difference. We want to pat ourselves on the back and feel proud of our accomplishments; we want bragging rights on our success and our impact.

In fact, this is essential to our wellbeing. Martin Seligman, one of the fathers of positive psychology, cites 'accomplishment' as the fifth piece in the puzzle that underpins the science of wellbeing. Seligman's research team found that, along with the essentials of positive emotion, engagement, positive relationships and meaning, we need to feel a sense of achievement to truly thrive. Importantly, many of us feel the need to tick off our own Big-ticket Life Items in order to define ourselves and establish our identity as someone who matters.

But, at the same time, we want to feel comfortable. We enjoy feeling safe and secure and, sometimes, our comfort zone is much more appealing than the alternative. Deep down, we know that it's easier to maintain the status quo and follow the path most travelled.

Less risk.

Less pain.

Less fear.

So herein lies the dilemma. How can we make a meaningful impact on the world without getting awkwardly uncomfortable?

The simple answer is: *we can't*.

Making an impact that changes lives and positively affects the planet involves stepping into our own power, owning our 'stuff' and being brave. It also requires tolerating ambiguity, sitting with free-floating anxiety and trusting our own instincts.

But this is not necessarily an either/or scenario. It's not about giving up all security, throwing caution to the wind and jumping off a cliff without a parachute. Nor is it about fearfully skimming the surface of our potential. It is about finding the balance between the two, building our resilience toolkit and setting ourselves up for success through smart, strategic choices and courageous action.

The key to navigating our way towards meaningful impact is found in three powerful C words:

Confidence, Courage and Competence.

These critical tools, when used together as building blocks for performance, have the capacity to shift us from 'I wish' to 'I did'. Self-confidence and courageous action enable us to draw on emotional intelligence, strategic knowledge and (importantly) well-developed instinct to make the right moves and ultimately make a positive impact.

So, how does it work?

First, let's understand how it does *not* work.

Courageous action without self-confidence often leads to superficial and temporary results. People with this profile tend to 'jump first, plan second'; they are all about being seen to do the high-profile thing without having the underpinning self-awareness, self-esteem or genuine belief in their own ability to sustain their results. When faced with obstacles, they crumble, lacking the basic resilience or authentic connections to support their growth. Sometimes, this can lead to the much-debated Imposter Syndrome – a psychological pattern where an individual doubts their accomplishments and has a persistent internalised fear of being exposed as a fraud. When we put ourselves in a situation that challenges our skills and resources without knowing that we can nail it or believing that we deserve it, it's no wonder that we end up a ball of anxiety.

Self-confidence without courageous action inevitably leads to labels like 'all talk, no action' or 'all sizzle, no sausage' or even 'all fur coat, no knickers'. You get the picture; it's about lacking substance or

Confidence, Courage and Competence:

when used together

THEY HAVE THE CAPACITY

to shift us from

'I wish' to 'I did'.

missing the willingness to demonstrate ability through action. While people with this profile can often make a positive initial impression, they soon become unravelled when they fail to deliver or deliver unimpressive results.

When someone has low self-confidence and is unlikely to take courageous action, they can become stuck in a rut at best or immobilised at worst. This is the profile of someone who has a low level of belief that they can achieve results and little belief that they actually deserve to. This is someone who is fearful of moving beyond their comfort zone and hesitant to take on any challenges that might expose them.

So, essentially, the ideal profile is to have robust self-confidence and strong readiness to take courageous action. This is where the potential to make a meaningful impact begins to exponentially grow. As we start to draw on our past successes and believe that we have the capacity to influence events, our sense of worthiness and capacity to see ourselves as successful builds. This self-confidence feeds into our motivation to take risks, to broaden our sphere of comfort and to step into our power as a flexible, agile agent of change. And, when this chosen action is aligned with personal values and beliefs, we are well on the path towards our full human potential.

This is how we can make a meaningful impact on our life and the lives of others.

BUT . . . WHO AM I TO LEAD YOU INTO CONFIDENCE?

You might be wondering what gives me the right to talk to you about confidence.

I have spent 20 years as a psychologist, 15 years as a corporate consultant, ten years as a personal and career coach and seven years in the media. These days I mainly focus on media projects and working with a select group of women like you.

Every new chapter in my career and life has started with one courageous step. From an early age, I discovered a passion for pushing myself outside my comfort zone and testing my own limits (I know, not everyone enjoys this!). I learned very early on that if I was going to live an extraordinary life – which I knew I wanted to do – I needed to break old patterns and do things differently. I needed to not just meet, but exceed the expectations of others and show them that I was not 'just a dreamer'.

And I showed them.

As a kid, all I ever wanted to do was work in TV and, now, here I am with a full-time career in the media.

But it wasn't easy.

I was often told to 'calm down' and 'slow down'. Maybe it was tall poppy syndrome or maybe my drive and ambition just made other people feel uncomfortable. I'm not sure why people didn't believe in my HUGE goals. But I did.

The resistance from others just strengthened my resolve. I became determined to prove them wrong and, gradually, I began to internalise my own steely belief.

Underestimate me. That'll be fun.
– ANONYMOUS

Over years of mistakes, failures and knock-backs, these were my key lessons:

- I learned that these things are just feedback, just data to inform future decisions.
- I developed a naturally optimistic outlook on life. I now genuinely see the glass as half full (even when those around me are screaming that it's half empty).

- My view of myself became one of clear, comfortable capability (three more C words) – I began to calmly believe that I could actually achieve anything I wanted to.
- I developed a highly flexible approach to obstacles, seeing them as temporary and changeable.
- I built more patience, though I'm still in the process of this . . . patience doesn't come so naturally to me. #workinprogress

These lessons have enabled me to build an airtight positive mindset, a healthy relationship with risk-taking, an unwavering self-belief and a dream career. Not to mention I met my perfect life-partner at 39 and had my gorgeous daughter, Maddie, at the age of 42. I've just turned 50 and, I couldn't be happier.

And now I'm here to show you how to do the same.

THE C WORD METHOD

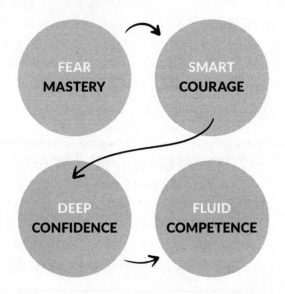

So, what is the C Word Method all about?

It is essentially your roadmap out of fear and into your own spotlight. I developed the C Word Method after years of research, study and supporting women to achieve their goals. It's the culmination of my work as a psychologist and personal coach – and of my own life experiences. In this book I will guide you through each stage of the method – you can see them in the image above. Let's touch on the four stages now.

Before your confidence journey can begin, you need to start with **Fear Mastery**. Fear, in and of itself, is not a bad thing. In fact, you'll discover that it performs a critical role in your life. But, of course, it can also act as a roadblock to your progress, a force that inhibits your development. So, we will begin by unpacking the role fear plays in your life and learning how to put it in its place.

Once this is achieved, you can up-level your life.

Before you can build confidence you must start taking courageous action. Expanding your comfort zone and taking some risks will lead you towards confidence. But **Smart Courage** is more than just making bold moves – it's about demonstrating *emotional bravery* and showing *intellectual savviness.*

There are many myths about confidence and it is often lumped together with traits like arrogance, cockiness, narcissism and showing off. But real **Deep Confidence** goes beyond the outward display of boldness and draws on genuine *self-esteem* and *self-efficacy.*

When authentic Deep Confidence is established, you will start to fly!

The most telling sign that someone is truly confident can be found in their performance results – in their career, their relationships and their life. Genuinely confident people tend to demonstrate **Fluid Competence**.

Have you ever watched someone performing a task and thought to yourself 'OMG, she makes it look so easy!'?

She was probably in a state psychologists call 'flow'. This state tends to happen when people are *strengths driven* and have *clarity of purpose*. This is Fluid Competence.

WHEN AUTHENTIC

Deep Confidence

is established,

YOU WILL START TO FLY!

We will unpack all of these concepts together in the pages of this book. I'll share some of my stories and life lessons, introduce you to some of my clients and give you the tools you need to get out of your own way and start to soar.

And I'll be suggesting some activities for you to practise so be prepared to take some (emotionally brave and intellectually savvy) risks.

This book will be your roadmap to the *biggest, boldest and most authentically confident version of you*. You will find you take more risks, enjoy challenges, improve your positive self-talk, reflect and learn from mistakes, embrace confidence and, essentially, transform your life into the life you've always wanted.

Let's do this.

Journal time

I believe there are two keys to unlocking sustainable cognitive, emotional and behavioural change:

- self-reflection
- rehearsal.

So, I've included a number of 'journal time' activities for you throughout *The C Word*. To get the most out of this book and increase your chances of creating long-term transformation in your life, I highly recommend you get a journal and take time with each activity as you read. You may prefer an old-school pen and book or perhaps you're more of a digital girl and opt to download a journalling app. Do whatever works for you.

part
one

Fear Mastery

FEAR
MASTERY

SMART
COURAGE

DEEP
CONFIDENCE

FLUID
COMPETENCE

You gain strength, courage and confidence by every experience in which you really stop to look fear in the face. You are able to say to yourself, 'I have lived through this horror. I can take the next thing that comes along.' You must do the thing you think you cannot do.

ELEANOR ROOSEVELT

Mastering fear is one of those critical life skills they should have taught us at school. Understanding what fear is, why it occurs and how you can manage it is critical to building a solid incubator for your confidence to grow within. In this section of the book, I'm going to pull the curtain back on fear and expose it for what it really is – just a series of (often irrational) thoughts and beliefs that lead to an unhelpful series of emotional and behavioural reactions.

Got Imposter Syndrome? We'll tackle it.

Guilty of listening to your unhelpful inner voice? We'll sort it.

Break into a sweat at the idea of a first date, public-speaking engagement or job interview? I've got you.

And I'm going to introduce you to some incredible people who have overcome fear-based obstacles in their everyday lives in order to flourish. The lessons you'll learn from them will truly change your outlook on your own capacity for change, adaptability, resilience and growth – they certainly changed mine.

FEAR
MASTERY

CHAPTER 1

FEAR
is not
YOUR FRENEMY

**(EVEN THOUGH IT FEELS LIKE SHE'S
RIPPING YOUR HEART OUT)**

Picture this: I'm in my late twenties doing my post-grad at uni and living my best life in a share-house in Hawthorn, Melbourne. Not a care in the world, I'm comfortable in my own skin, I enjoy living in a free country and my daily existence is pretty calm and non-threatening. One evening I decide to indulge in a relaxing bubble bath. After a long day in the uni lab, I can't wait to switch off my brain and sink into the silky water, surrounded by nothing but soothing music, my hopes and dreams.

Totally naked save for the bright pink floral shower cap on my head, I decide to sit on the loo for a quick wee before the bath. As I sit, I start singing along in my loudest voice, with my most passionate face, 'I am woman, hear me roar!' Bliss. Still seated, I turn my head and look at the window above the bath. What I see destroys my mood and changes my experience of baths for years to come.

A peeping tom.

There he is, taking in the scene of me, naked, singing and wearing a pink floral cap. Sh*t.

I quickly bolted from the bathroom to alert my housemate, Fiona, and call my dad (a detective senior sergeant in the Victoria Police at the time). After a stiff drink and a few hysterical laughing fits, Fiona and I eventually calmed down and put it all in perspective. But I'll never forget it.

•

Have you ever had one of these 'OMG, my life is about to end' moments? One of those times when your life flashed before your eyes, the ground dropped out from under you and you were sucked into a vortex of terror?

Good. That means you're alive!

If you can, I want you to hold your memory of a time like this in your mind's eye as you read this chapter. I'm not being cruel – this will help you to really understand (at a visceral level) what fear is about, why we have it and, most importantly, how to move past it.

Deal?

Fear is normal.

But it does not have to be your frenemy – that enemy cleverly disguised as a friend.

Fear exists for a reason. It is an innate response that we have developed to protect ourselves from danger or threats. Depending on the threat, fear can be a physical response, such as your heart racing, or a psychological response, such as intense anxiety.

From an evolutionary perspective, our ancestors developed the fear response as a critical survival tactic. When faced with a threat to themselves, their families or their food source, it was essential that they defend themselves. So, their ingenious brains and bodies would switch *on* some bodily functions and switch *off* others.

The fear response would boost the activity in the heart and lungs for extra energy (thus the 'racing heart' feeling), dilate pupils and create tunnel vision for clearer focus, and send extra blood to the hands and feet for additional dexterity (this can feel like 'pins and needles').

At the same time, activity in the stomach and intestines would reduce (thus the feeling of 'butterflies'), and tears and saliva would be inhibited (thus the dry mouth), all to avoid wasting energy on non-essential functions. Hearing would be minimised to allow greater focus on sight.

So, the brain and body worked together to build survival mechanisms to keep the species safe. Fast-forward to the present day and the brain has not evolved much more. This is why you might notice you can be a little 'trigger happy' when it comes to your own fear response.

And, as I'm sure you can imagine, I *always* check the bathroom window when I'm on the loo.

WHAT ARE WE REALLY SCARED OF?

When we break it down, our fear reactions are all about our perception of risk or, sometimes, our misperceptions.

David Ropeik, the Director of Risk Communication at the Harvard Center for Risk Analysis, has conducted some fascinating research into the consequences of fear. He notes that:

> our modern apprehensions are in part an outgrowth of the post–World War Two industrial–technological–information age that has given us both the benefits and the risks of everything from plastics to pesticides, nuclear power to mobile phones, biotechnology to global travel, and more.[1]

While we have more global connectivity and technologically enabled luxuries in the contemporary developed world, we also experience the associated new risks that feed our fears and anxieties.

Ropeik's 2004 study of risk perception identified that our 'responses to risks are not simply internal "rational" risk analyses, but also intuitive "affective" responses that apply our emotions, values and instincts as we try to judge danger'.[2]

This goes a long way to explaining why our fears don't always match the facts.

Ever been told you're 'making a mountain out of a molehill'? Your fear may not be based on the factual measurements of said molehill, but rather your emotional response to your instincts, attitudes and beliefs about the little mound. Thus, you may actually experience it as a mountain – this is your reality and your subsequent decisions and behaviours will be dictated by this.

PERCEPTION IS REALITY

According to Ropeik's research, we are likely to interpret the risk of a situation based on a number of subjective factors:

- **Trust** – The more trust we feel in the people, institutions, culture or situations associated with a risk, the less fear we will experience.

- **Dread** – A risk that might harm or even kill you in a *dreadful* way seems much scarier than one that might impact you more subtly. For instance, although the data shows that heart disease kills more people than cancer, more people report a sense of dread about dying from cancer. It seems that risks that have a higher 'drama' factor are seen as more dangerous, and no doubt the media have a role to play here.

- **Control** – When we feel more in control of a situation, we tend to experience less fear. You might think twice next time you consider calling someone a control freak – they are probably doing what they can to increase their feeling of control over their environment and minimise their perception of risk, and therefore reduce the fear in their life. #bekind

- **Natural or human-made** – The research found that 'unnatural' interventions tend to evoke a greater fear response than those that happen naturally. So, you might be more suspicious of food genetically modified in a lab than a new plant variety derived from naturally occurring cross-pollination.

- **Choice** – A risk we actively choose feels like it poses less danger than a risk imposed upon us. Understandably, we feel more comfortable (and more in control) when we choose to step into risk of our own free will.

- **Children** – We are evolutionarily wired to protect our offspring so a risk affecting children is at the top of our risk hierarchy. This may explain the dramatic response to low-level risks such as traces of mercury in fish.

- **Uncertainty** – The more uncertain we are, the more cautious and fearful we become. Our brain likes to 'fill in the gaps' when we don't have all the information and, often, this takes the form of worst-case scenarios.
- **Novelty** – New risks (such as COVID-19) tend to frighten us more than those we have lived with for a while, which we may have put into perspective.
- **Awareness** – The more aware we are of a risk, the greater fear we experience. So, when our newsfeeds are filled with stories of child abductions, our caution and anxiety around our children goes through the roof.
- **Could it happen to me?** – We are likely to experience greater fear of something if we believe it could happen to us or someone we know or love.
- **The risk-benefit trade-off** – What are we likely to gain from taking this risk? If we believe the pay-off may be worth it, we are more likely to take the risk. This is often seen in financial investments, where evidence of good returns can be very persuasive in our willingness to part with our hard-earned cash.
- **Catastrophic or chronic?** – We are more afraid of catastrophic incidents that kill a large number of people, such as a plane crash, than long-term risks, such as heart disease.[3]

This research provides strong support for the idea that fear is in our minds. Now, I don't mean this in a dismissive way or to minimise our experience of fear at all – quite the contrary. It reminds us that, regardless of the cold hard facts, our experience of fear is a direct response to our perception of risk, our emotional reaction to that risk and our lived experience.

So, if you have experience with fear (and her close cousin, anxiety) I have good news for you. You don't have to sit in fear and endure the emotional load that comes along for the ride.

You have a choice.

You don't have to keep choosing fear.

You can choose freedom.

YOU ARE THE MISTRESS OF YOUR MIND (AND THE REST, AS THEY SAY, IS HERSTORY)

I'd like to introduce you to what I believe is one of the greatest contributions the science of psychology has made to the quality of modern life: Cognitive Behavioural Therapy (CBT).

It's smart, efficient, logical and easy to implement. While it's not a cure-all and is often only one part of the puzzle in complex mental health treatment plans, when it comes to walking the line between *functioning* and *flourishing* in 'normal life', CBT is incredibly powerful.

CBT is one of the few approaches to therapy that puts the client (in this case, YOU) squarely in the driver's seat. By learning CBT strategies and methods, you gain control over the direction of your life. You discover that you have the capacity to promote transformational change in your life and you feel empowered to do so.

To break it down, CBT centres on the delicate relationship between our thoughts, feelings and behaviour. Essentially, it teaches us that our thoughts create our feelings and our feelings drive our behaviour. Thus, if we can recognise and change our unhelpful thoughts (that is, our perceptions of our world) then we can have a significant impact on the decisions we make and the direction our life ultimately takes.

For me, CBT is very much about personal responsibility. It's about owning your internal monologue, warts and all, and taking accountability for the impact your own thoughts have on your emotional life and lived experience.

CBT teaches us that we are not victims – we are smart, empowered people with agency, free will and an abundance of choice. We just have to do the work.

Let's take a closer look.

THE SCENARIO

You woke late this morning because you accidentally set the alarm on your phone for pm instead of am. This immediately got your heart racing as you knew you had an important meeting at 9am. As you jumped out of bed you stepped on the cat and he yelped out in pain (both his *and* your hair stood on end!).

Racing into the bathroom, you stubbed your toe on the doorframe and squealed as pain throbbed through your entire foot. Halfway through your shower, with a head-full of conditioner, the hot water ran out and there you were – freezing, stressed and rinsing the slimy liquid off your shivering head.

Eventually making it to the kitchen, you quickly grabbed your favourite cereal and attempted to pour on the milk. Only it didn't pour, it slopped. Chunky off-milk.

As you drove towards your workplace, a spider leapt across your dashboard, giving you one almighty fright. You froze, instinctively slamming on the brakes and causing another car to crash right up your rear. You were not physically hurt, but, by the same token, you were definitely not having a great start to your day.

What happened next?

Response 1 – *the unhelpful voice*

Let's assume you have an automatic, unhelpful line of thought running through your mind:

- **Thoughts** – You tell yourself things like 'I'm such a loser', 'I can't even drive right', 'This is the worst day ever', 'I'm hopeless', 'I should have stayed in bed', 'I can't do anything right', 'This car is going to cost me a fortune and it's all my fault'.
- **Feelings** – You experience emotions such as shame, embarrassment, guilt, frustration, anger, defeat, loss and distress.

- **Actions** – As a result, you engage in the following behaviours: you burst into tears, yell at the other driver and blame them for the accident, forget which insurance agency you're with, lose your phone resulting in extreme panic for three minutes, almost step out in front of traffic and eventually drive off without exchanging details with the other driver. You arrive at work highly agitated, flustered and anything but ready to step into that important meeting. Uh oh.

Response 2 – the helpful voice

However, if you were to engage in a more considered, helpful internal monologue:

- **Thoughts** – You tell yourself things like 'Oh no! But it's okay, no one is hurt', 'This is so frustrating but at least I have good insurance', 'Well, now I know how quick my reflexes are!', 'Everything is okay, it's just a minor incident and that spider was out of my control', 'Now I have an excuse to get a new car!'
- **Feelings** – You experience emotions such as frustration and moderate stress but also some relief, focus, gratitude and even a little inspiration.
- **Actions** – As a result, you engage in the following behaviours: you put things in perspective and, with a relatively clear head, you engage openly with the other driver and make sure both cars are safe from oncoming traffic; you examine both cars, exchange car and insurance details, make plans to deal with the administrative aspects of the incident and cautiously make your way to work. You arrive at work certainly a little rattled, but also relatively calm with a funny story to share.

As you probably figured out, the first thinking pattern put you into a state of fight, flight or freeze (AKA survival mode). You were flooded with adrenaline and cortisol (the stress hormone) and this physiological state robbed you of your capacity to stay calm, think clearly, remember critical details, solve problems effectively or have positive, constructive interactions during a high-stress situation.

If you take a close look at the second thinking pattern and subsequent outcome, you might describe it as the *opposite* of fight, flight or freeze. Wouldn't we all prefer to take the approach in the second scenario?

REFRAMING FEAR

The REALLY interesting thing about the fear reaction in your body is that it is very similar to your experience of excitement (biologically speaking). Studies suggest that a major factor in how humans experience fear has to do with the *context* (or the story we tell ourselves about the situation).

A quick brain hack can change your entire experience of a situation: this requires over-riding your emotional brain with a clear, strong message from your rational brain. Telling yourself 'I'm excited' can be a powerful antidote to an internal monologue that's playing 'I'm scared' on repeat.

This means that if you become highly attuned to your own inner world, you can start to take control of your emotions and therefore your lived experience. If you get really well-acquainted with your self-talk (your thinking brain), then you can start to make some shifts that will impact the way you feel and experience your life (your emotional brain).

In real terms, this means that when you start to notice the early warning signs of fear in your body and behaviour, you can convert the fear to excitement and have a completely different experience.

Sounds simple enough. But . . . how?

SELF-AWARENESS

Before you can influence the type of lived experience you have, you must first delve into your *thinking brain* and try to understand the current state of play.

**Self-awareness is the first step in changing
your experience of fear.**

How do YOU know when you're in a fear state? What happens inside YOUR body? Inside YOUR mind? It's different for everyone, so it's important for you to get to know your own personal fear response.

When you consider the fight, flight or freeze description of the fear responses, which one do you tend to favour when you're in an uncomfortable situation?

Go back to that frightful memory I asked you about earlier – what did you DO when the fear set in?

1. Did you stand up, ready to battle the source of your fright?
2. Did you run away?
3. Did you stop, frozen on the spot?

Although it can be a confronting and scary experience to go through something like this, it's actually really helpful to you. This experience has provided you with meaningful data that you can work with: by knowing your natural response to fear – that is, the fight, flight or freeze response – you can be more mindful and prepared for future events.

Now, this is not to say I recommend you walk around feeling 'ready' for something bad to happen (we all know about self-fulfilling prophecies). Rather, by being aware of how you usually respond in scary situations, if and when something does happen you'll experience less anxiety because you'll know what to expect.

But of course, fear isn't just one general response. You experience it at a granular, personal level too. It's a great idea to conduct a self-audit of the specific responses you tend to demonstrate because, once again, this will reduce your anxiety in the face of fear.

Some of the common **physical** reactions to fear include:
- sweating, perhaps in places where you don't usually sweat
- uncontrollable shaking
- hot flushes or cold flushes (AKA chills)
- short, shallow breathing or having trouble catching your breath
- feeling as though your throat is closing and you're about to choke
- racing or irregular heartbeat
- feeling tightness in your chest, like someone is squeezing your heart
- upset stomach, like butterflies or nausea
- the rapid onset of a headache (more intense than normal headaches)
- feeling dizzy, perhaps like you're going to faint
- fingers and toes becoming numb (this might feel like pins and needles)
- your mouth becomes dry, saliva temporarily stops producing
- a desperate need to go to the toilet
- your ears have an intense sensation, like a ringing, which can become quite loud and distracting.

Do any of these symptoms sound familiar?

And then, there are the less talked-about behavioural reactions to fear, sometimes called *defensive behaviours*.

When you anticipate or experience a threat, what do you do? How do you communicate? What happens to the tone and volume of your voice? How do your posture and gestures change? What happens to your general demeanour?

Here are some of the common **behavioural** reactions to fear. Try them on for size and see if any of them fit. Because behavioural reactions to fear are not always, shall we say, 'socially positive', these may be behaviours of yours that others have complained to you about.

I know this is a sensitive topic, but think about situations where you've received critical feedback about your behaviour and ask yourself, 'Was I feeling fearful at the time?' Perhaps you:

- lost your sense of humour (ever been called a Debbie Downer?)
- quickly took offence at something that may have been quite benign
- insisted you were 'right' without listening to alternative points of view
- had to have the last word, even if it meant unnecessarily carrying on an argument
- flooded someone with information or evidence to prove your point (AKA information overkill)
- kept explaining and rationalising, even after your point was made
- stepped into the victim role and played 'poor me'
- started sounding like a preacher, teacher or parent
- lost your capacity to be flexible and became rigid and closed off to alternative ideas with no interest in negotiating
- went into denial and refused to accept that something was happening
- turned your back on the situation and refused to engage
- communicated with sarcasm or cynicism
- became 'mean', blaming anyone but yourself and being overly critical of others
- used excuses like 'I'm just being 100 per cent honest' or 'It's just how I am, that's my personality'
- became overly and inauthentically 'nice', using a false smile and insincere niceties.

How many of these defensive behaviours do you recognise?

Journal time

MY FEAR RESPONSES

Create two columns on the page with the headings:
- Physical
- Behavioural

Holding your memory of that scary event I asked you to think about earlier in your mind, jot down everything you can remember *happening to your body.* Use the list above as a guide.

Then, try to recall all the *things you did.* How did you behave? What choices or decisions did you make in fear? How did you communicate with others? What changed in your demeanour?

CHANGING THE MEANING OF FEAR

Remember I mentioned the concept that fear and excitement are experienced very similarly within our bodies? Well, it's often called the 'stress reflex' and as well as cropping up when you feel threatened, it's how you can respond to exciting events too.

- About to walk on stage? Heart beats faster, sweat flows, stomach gets butterflies, throat feels dry.
- Ready to ask your crush out? Heart beats faster, sweat flows, stomach gets butterflies, throat feels dry, tummy rumbles.
- Preparing for your wedding day? Heart beats faster, sweat flows, stomach gets butterflies, throat feels dry, tummy rumbles, possibly vomit.

Notice any similarities between these symptoms and those in your own list of fear responses?

**Although the external stimuli are different,
the internal reactions you have are similar.**

Your body simply responds to your *interpretation* of the event.

This means that you have control over your experience of fear – and whether it becomes a difficult, distressing experience or just a little frustration. You can choose to attach a different meaning to the experience.

You can label it differently.

It is possible to transform *dysfunctional* fear into something more constructive. I'm talking about the type of fear that doesn't serve you, rather than the useful fear that appears when you face a legitimate threat (this fear is there for a good reason – it keeps you safe).

A series of psychological experiments conducted in 2014 provided empirical evidence that dysfunctional fears can be mastered and showed some awesome fear-reducing results![4] It turns out that if you are feeling those fear-related physical sensations, an effective way of taking control of your mental state is as simple as saying out loud: 'I'm feeling excited' or 'I'm getting excited about . . .' (fill in the blank with the formerly fear-inducing situation).

Sounds *simple*. And it is. Simple, but not *easy*.

So how do you do it?

Before you can master the linguistic reprogramming mentioned above, it helps to have a strategy in place to reduce the intensity of your fear first. One way is to let the worst-case scenario play out like a movie in your mind. This is to help you push past the worst-case scenario and see yourself reach a safe conclusion, an ending where you survived and are safe. Take a few minutes to try this exercise:

> Give yourself some time and space to get comfortable, without distractions. Take three deep, slow, intentional breaths and close your eyes. Allow yourself to feel comfortable and safe. Now, play out the worst-case scenario like a movie in your mind – imagine the thing you fear happening. Let it play out,

allow all the possibilities to come into play, let the consequences evolve. Just let it happen. Don't hit 'pause' at the most difficult part, let it play out and then, before it finishes, *intentionally* direct it to a safe ending.

Try this process a few times until you are comfortable that the situation is not as bad as you first thought. By playing it out in your mind, you'll start to see and believe that you *can* find different solutions to your fear-based problems. When you feel more at ease with the situation, try saying out loud, 'I'm excited about . . .' whatever your situation is. Say it to other people, post it on social media, and talk openly and often about your experience of excitedly anticipating the event. Notice how different this feels.

Say it again: I'm excited about

_____.

In order to understand how to overcome fear, it's important to consider your end game.

That is, courage. Let's take a look at some great examples of courage in history:

- Anne Frank and her family living in secret to hide from the Nazis
- Rosa Parks refusing to give up her seat on the bus
- Martin Luther King Jr standing up for equal rights
- Joan of Arc facing harsh criticism and burning at the stake for her beliefs
- the police, firefighters and citizens who rushed into the World Trade Center to save lives on September 11, 2001
- our first responders and medical staff fighting to protect us all from the deadly risks of COVID-19.

What do all of these heroes have in common?

They were all working towards a higher good, a bigger picture, a long-term endgame. They all had an *ultimate mission* that was so important to them, it outshone any experience of fear.

Pause and think about that for a moment.

Say this in your mind or out loud: COURAGE emerges when what you WANT is bigger than what you FEAR.

Journal time

MY COURAGE BALANCE SHEET

I'd like you to go back into your memory and select a time when you demonstrated courage. If you feel comfortable, relive it with as much colour and vividness as you can.

Then, create two columns on the page with the headings:

* What I feared
* What I wanted

Holding the memory of your courageous behaviour in your mind, write down everything you can remember from that time for each category.

Now, give each item in both columns an importance rating out of 10.

It will likely become clear to you that your goal or mission for this situation *outweighed* your fear. This is what *enabled* you to demonstrate courage.

What does this teach you about courage?

I suppose you may now be wondering, 'Hmm, now she's on about courage. Where is the confidence?' Fair call.

**In order to be confident, you first need
to be courageous. In order to be courageous,
you first need to overcome fear.**

So, it stands to reason that, as part of our confidence journey together, we need to first pay homage to fear (so that we can kick her in the guts), then move into the courageous space. Courage is where you will build the foundations for your confidence to blossom, courage is the state that will enable you to move from where you are now to where you want to be.

LET'S GET PRACTICAL

So far, we've discovered that an important part of the fear-courage-confidence-competence journey is self-awareness. To ease you into the self-analysis process, I thought I'd begin by giving you the opportunity to analyse someone else – it's always easier to be objective about someone else rather than ourselves, right?

To set the scene, I'm introducing you to a fictional character named Danni. Danni is a single 30-something heterosexual woman who describes herself as having a fear of dating. This fear seems to get in the way whenever she puts herself out there. She really wants to find a great partner and settle into a loving relationship, but somehow she always manages to self-sabotage. Danni has decided to face her fear head-on and is going to a bar by herself tonight.

Journal time

ANALYSE DANNI

Danni nervously entered her favourite inner city bar and ordered a lychee martini. 'I can do this!' she told herself as she awkwardly wriggled onto the bar stool. She knew she needed to overcome her fear of meeting new people, but why did she have to choose a bar to do it in? She felt conspicuous, like everyone was staring at her (and not in a good way). For years, Danni had felt like an outsider, especially when it came to her relationships with men. As a kid, she was always a little socially awkward, never quite getting the jokes and never really understanding the 'vibe' of the other kids. Sure, she was book smart, but when it came to making friends and being accepted, she always seemed to fall short.

Attempting to appear confident as she drank the last drop of her cocktail, Danni casually peered around the bar and offered a *combination hair-flick and giggle* for anyone who cared to observe.

She noticed the guy sitting near her at the bar. 'Oh, he's gorgeous – that jawline, those biceps . . . but I'm sure he won't even notice me.'

Then, before she knew it, he turned to her. 'I'm Rob,' he said. 'Can I buy you a drink?'

Danni was overcome by unhelpful thoughts: 'I'm so awkward and unrefined and he's clearly a total gentleman. If I have a drink with him it will only take ten minutes before he realises I'm a complete fraud. I shouldn't embarrass myself anymore, I'll make an excuse and get away now.'

Danni was so close to leaving right then and there, but, remembering why she'd come to the bar in the first place, said, 'Um, I've been drinking lychee martinis.'

Without missing a beat, Rob ordered them a martini each and paid with a crisp $100 note.

The sight of the note was enough to send Danni's heart racing. 'He's loaded and obviously out of my league,' she thought, her breathing becoming faster and shallower.

How absolutely embarrassing.

Rob moved seats so he was sitting right next to Danni, almost close enough for their knees to touch.

That was enough to start up her unhelpful thinking again. 'Oh god, he's going to notice my knees shaking and he'll know I'm totally out of my depth. He's so close he'll see that pimple I tried to conceal – argh, it feels massive. I wonder if

I have BO, but I can't check without being totally obvious. Did I clean my teeth before I left, I can't remember, I probably have tragic breath. I really don't deserve this stunning man's attention . . . What if I . . .? How can I . . .? I have to . . .'

Before she realised what she was doing, Danni quickly stood up, turned without saying a word to Rob and ran out of the bar.

•

Consider these questions and write your responses in your journal:

- What were Danni's fears? Can you identify the difference between her deep fears and more superficial fears?
- How realistic were her fears? Was there any evidence to support them?
- How did her fears influence her self-talk?
- What was the emotional impact of having those thoughts?
- How satisfied would she have been with the outcome of leaving the bar when she did?

Now, let's give Danni a helping hand. I think we'll all agree that she could benefit from reframing her thinking. As we know by now, changing your thinking will change your feelings and this will, in turn, change your experience and outcomes in life.

We begin by exchanging her fear-based, unhelpful thoughts for more rational, realistic, *mildly optimistic* thoughts.

Are you wondering why I've said 'mildly optimistic' and haven't suggested we simply swap negative thoughts for positive thoughts? Well, first, because humans are nuanced and complicated and our experience is rarely this binary, but also because our brains are very cluey! If Danni were to make the grand leap to 'I'm the most beautiful woman in the room, any man would be lucky to have me', what do you think would happen? Her rational brain would probably reject this thought outright, thus undermining the whole process. It's better to move from negative/*unhelpful* thoughts to neutral/mildly optimistic/*helpful* thoughts as they will be more congruent with your mindset and more likely to be believed.

So back to Danni. Here's an example of how she might reframe her thinking:

THOUGHTS

INITIAL THOUGHT	REFRAMED THOUGHT
'I'm so awkward and unrefined, he is a total gentleman and if I have a drink with him it will take ten minutes before he realises I'm a complete fraud, I shouldn't embarrass myself any further . . . must make an excuse and get away NOW!'	'I'm nervous but I guess that's to be expected, and he might be nervous too. He is very attractive and I know I look my best tonight. I have as much right to sit with him as any other woman in the room. I deserve this!'

As you can tell, Danni has removed the fear from the equation while acknowledging that a little nervousness is completely normal. She uses new language that supports her self-esteem, reinforcing her worth without being inauthentic. It is likely that her rational brain will accept this without too much dissonance (that is, confusion about conflicting thoughts).

Once her reframed thoughts are embedded, we can expect her emotional state to follow suit:

FEELINGS

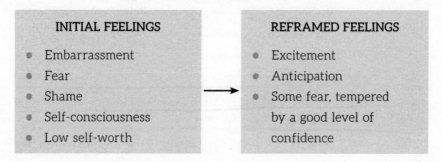

INITIAL FEELINGS	REFRAMED FEELINGS
• Embarrassment	• Excitement
• Fear	• Anticipation
• Shame	• Some fear, tempered
• Self-consciousness	by a good level of
• Low self-worth	confidence

Once again, we do not expect her to suddenly experience off-the-charts confidence levels, but her emotional state has shifted from one of self-doubt to one of self-acceptance (with a side of mild excitement).

This lighter emotional state is likely to flow through to her behaviour:

BEHAVIOURS

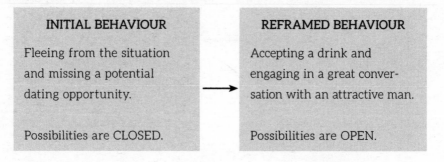

INITIAL BEHAVIOUR	REFRAMED BEHAVIOUR
Fleeing from the situation and missing a potential dating opportunity.	Accepting a drink and engaging in a great conversation with an attractive man.
Possibilities are CLOSED.	Possibilities are OPEN.

As you can see, the clearest difference between the two outcomes is the openness to possibilities. I'm sure Danni would be proud of herself for staying and sharing a drink with Rob. I wonder what happened next?

•

I hope you're starting to see that fear does not have to be your frenemy. Fear is simply a set of thoughts and feelings that automatically emerge when we are faced with a threat. Reframing is the smart tool you need to take control of fear-based thoughts and exchange them for a more rational, helpful mindset.

Courage

emerges when what you want *is bigger* than what YOU FEAR.

CHAPTER 2

BE THE

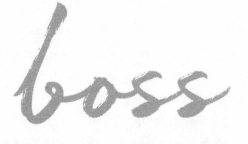

OF YOUR
IMPOSTER

I have a fabulous coaching client who is a high-flying, achievement-focused single woman with a flourishing international career (let's call her Malia). Widely considered an expert in her field, she flies all over the globe for speaking engagements, lectures at top universities, consults to high-profile companies and has won several awards for innovation. She even shares her expertise with a select group of elite athletes, business leaders and celebrities. You might say, she's made it.

I recently sat down with Malia for a coffee and catch-up after one of her many successful assignments. As she related her project to me, she was animated, energised and clearly proud of her achievement. Objectively speaking, she had kicked some serious goals (in a male-dominated sphere) and she had no problem describing the project in detail.

As we sipped our coffees, I pulled out my laptop for a quick live review of her website.

I have to tell you, I nearly dropped my coffee. At first, I thought I had arrived at the wrong site. I knew her branding needed an overhaul (this was why we were taking a look) but the information on her site gave *no indication* of her expertise or experience. There was literally no mention of her awards, university lecturing or the calibre of her international assignments. Malia's website was a bland representation of her baseline skills; it gave a vague nod to her qualifications but said nothing about her achievements.

When I asked her why there was such a chasm between her lived experience and her online presence she looked flat, defeated and suddenly quite sad.

'I can't put that stuff on my website,' she said.

'Why not?' I asked.

'People won't believe me. Or maybe they'll think I've exaggerated my experience or that I don't deserve to be at this level. I've been very lucky in my career and somehow have ended up at the right place at the right time. It's not really my achievements, it's just . . . you know . . . luck.'

ENTER: IMPOSTER SYNDROME

I'm sure you've heard about Imposter Syndrome by now; maybe you've even recognised some of the features in your own experience. It's a psychological term that describes the experience of doubting your abilities and achievements, and the fear that you are going to be exposed.

It's not an actual psychological disorder; the term was coined by clinical psychologists Pauline Clance and Suzanne Imes in 1978 when they found that people who demonstrated Imposter Syndrome tended to doubt their own achievements, despite clear evidence to the contrary. These people seemed to be convinced that they didn't deserve success, even though they had worked for it. And while it was once considered a 'women's problem' recent research has revealed that all genders experience Imposter Syndrome in approximately equal measures.

Imposter Syndrome is like having an invisible *negative filter* between yourself and the world – everything you see, hear and do is coloured by the theme 'I don't deserve this'.

One of the key features of this syndrome is the broken record of self-talk that plays on repeat: 'I'm a fraud, people think I'm smarter/more competent than I really am, I'm going to be exposed at any moment.'

Here are some common scenarios:

REALITY (What actually happened)	PERCEPTION (What you told yourself)
You have a great first date with an attractive person and they contact you to suggest a second date.	'Ha! They must have fallen for my "perfect girlfriend" routine and think I'm something I'm not. They have no idea I'm hopeless in relationships and probably expect me to live up to their outrageous expectations. I can't go on the second date, I'll be revealed as the undateable, terminally single loser I am.'

REALITY (What actually happened)	PERCEPTION (What you told yourself)
You get the career promotion you've been working towards for years.	'Oh no, I've managed to blag my way through the interview and now they expect me to actually do the job! They have no idea I've been faking my way through my career for years, but now I'm going to be exposed. I can't do this.'
You attend a parenting group with your first baby, and the other parents comment on how well your baby is thriving.	'Surely they can see I'm a mess! The only reason my baby is doing well is because my mother-in-law has been staying with us and because Bubs has strong genes. Her progress has nothing to do with me and I have no idea how I'm going to keep this parenting caper up – I feel like a kid dressed in adults' clothes.'

My work with Malia and many clients like her has taught me that there is often a clear disconnection between the reality (evidence) and the perception of the situation (belief system). One of the things we know about self-talk and the power of mindset is that *the stories we tell ourselves* define our experience.

Our eyes may see one thing, our ears hear it and our brains sense it, but our minds may interpret it differently and therefore create an experience that is not congruent with what we saw or heard.

It is, quite literally, a breakdown between reality and perception and it can unravel your relationships, career and life. It might seem absurd that people ignore blatant evidence in their world in favour of a fantasy-land version of reality, but, for many, this is more palatable.

For some people, the idea of owning their accomplishments and strengths is too confronting or shameful, and it's easier to play them down and give the credit to others.

**In many cases, what sits beneath the
Imposter Syndrome mindset is FEAR.**

This could be fear of:

- being less than perfect
- social or intimate rejection
- abandonment
- humiliation
- vulnerability
- success (yes, even success).

Before we get too heavy, I need to let you know that there is a silver lining here! It's not all doom, gloom and feeling like you're standing naked in a stadium full of judgmental doubters.

The good news is that *you* get to change the narrative – you have the opportunity to change the record playing on repeat in your mind. Yep, you are the mistress of your destiny and, now that we are here together, I'm going to show you how. Are you with me?

DAYDREAM YOUR WAY TO SUCCESS

You're about to step into the boardroom to present your case. After being recently promoted, this is your first time at the table. You try to rehearse your thoughts but they are overpowered by the daydream that is playing out in your mind in bright, vivid, living colour. In your mind, you walk into the room, open your mouth to speak and, before you get to say a word, the room erupts in a cacophony of 'Who is *she*?', 'She does not deserve to be here', 'She's just a kid', 'What does she know?' and, the kicker, 'She's a fraud!'

●

It's Imposter Syndrome at play. Some of you may relate to that sense of self-doubt, the feeling that you don't really deserve to be successful, that fear that at any moment you're going to be called out as a fraud.

If Meryl Streep and Tina Fey have reported experiencing Imposter Syndrome, surely it's understandable that we do too, right?

One of the things I learned during my 20 years as a psychologist is that fantasies matter. Self-talk is important as it generates emotions and action. Values and beliefs are important as they directly guide decisions and choices in life.

But your fantasies can fast-track your confidence and kick Imposter Syndrome to the curb – if you choose the right ones.

One of the underpinning features of Imposter Syndrome is what I call the **exposure fantasy**. This is a daydream where you are caught out, exposed, undone or revealed for the fraud you think you are. Unfortunately, our brains are still caught in the Dark Ages when it comes to scanning our environment for positive and negative cues, and we naturally select the negative over positive most of the time (as a primal way of keeping ourselves safe). So an exposure fantasy, or any other negative, fear-based fantasy, is likely to feel like a rather natural place for your mind to land, especially when you're anxious.

Be honest with yourself: have you ever experienced an exposure fantasy?

When you have these types of fantasies, you are sharpening your focus on the negative things in your environment and increasing your anxiety about something bad happening. This can send you into fight, flight or freeze mode, thus decreasing your capacity to stay calm, think clearly or perform to your potential.

Not surprisingly, this often becomes a self-fulfilling prophecy.

POSITIVE VISUALISATIONS

Let me share a (rather embarrassing) personal story with you. From as early as I can remember, I have been having **recognition fantasies**.

Whether I was completing a school exam, a dance class, a meeting or just walking down the street, the same fantasy theme would play out in my mind:

> I am discovered, recognised and celebrated for my amazing skills, attributes, talent and, sometimes, my awesome hair (hey, it's my fantasy – I can play it anyway I like). Sometimes I would be discovered by a Hollywood producer who would pluck me out of obscurity and into the movies; or the dance teacher would move me from the back to the front of the class so everyone could follow me; or my boss would make an announcement to the whole company that I had done amazing work and would be promoted; or the gorgeous man in the bar would cross the room to buy ME a drink.

For many years, I was ashamed of this automatic thinking pattern.

I felt that it was a sign that I was too confident or, as we Aussies say, 'up myself'. But as I got older and started putting myself in more and more challenging life situations, I realised that my recognition fantasies were, in fact, my secret weapon.

As I began studying and then practising psychology, I understood that I was naturally engaging in positive visualisations and building my confidence through a fantasised version of mental rehearsal.

TV DREAMS

I believe my ability to put myself out there and back myself is a direct result of my fantasy world.

The biggest example in my life is my TV career. I remember watching TV as a kid and mentally projecting myself onto the screen – I'd send photos into TV stations, enter competitions and call in whenever there was a telethon. I saw myself as a TV person for 40 years before it came to fruition, and that vision continues to this day.

YOUR FANTASIES

can fast-track your

confidence

and kick

Imposter Syndrome

to the curb –
if you choose
THE RIGHT ONES.

When it came to pitching myself to production companies and networks in recent years, it felt like a very natural, comfortable thing to do. Today, being in front of the camera has become my 'happy place'. #itreallyworks

MASTERING YOUR FANTASIES

So, how can you swap your exposure fantasies for recognition fantasies? Follow these four steps.

1. **Become self-aware** – The first step is learning to recognise *when* your exposure fantasies are happening. They usually creep up on you unconsciously and, before you know it, you're in the middle of a full-blown self-sabotaging disaster. It's a good idea to start by checking in with yourself at regular intervals each day. Set reminders in your phone for every three hours with the pop-up question 'What am I fantasising about?'

2. **Keep a journal** – Jot down the content of your unhelpful fantasies. Over a period of two weeks you'll likely start to see some patterns. This information will help you start to understand what is driving your thoughts, feelings and actions.

3. **Design your recognition fantasy** – Spend some time thinking about your biggest goals and life ambitions. Choose the one that is most important to you. In your journal, write about your fantasy of being recognised, discovered or highly successful in this area of your life. Write it like a story with as much colour and detail as you can muster. There are no rules or limits here and no one else is going to read it – really go for it. Once your recognition fantasy has become clear, summarise it in one powerful sentence. You can use this sentence as an affirmation to repeat often. Keep it somewhere private, but easily accessible to you.

4. **Stop and swap** – After practising for a while, you'll start to recognise an exposure fantasy *while* you're having it. Some people find it helpful to use a technique to signal to their brain that they mean business about stopping unhelpful thoughts: saying 'stop' or 'no' out loud or keeping a rubber band around your wrist and flicking it when the unhelpful thoughts emerge can be really powerful. This is where the gold is! Here is your opportunity to STOP the unhelpful fantasy and swap it for a more helpful, empowering fantasy. Whenever you find yourself having an exposure fantasy or unhelpful thoughts, repeat your fantasy affirmation and take a moment to play out the recognition fantasy in your mind.

Remember, you have a choice: you can change your thoughts, your feelings and, ultimately, your results.

> **The greatest weapon against stress is our ability to choose one thought over another.**
>
> **WILLIAM JAMES**

DON'T JUST CHANGE YOUR MIND, CHANGE YOUR BRAIN

One of the most exciting recent developments in neuroscience is the discovery that our brains are *elastic* – meaning they can change and evolve. Physically. This is called neuroplasticity.

Research on brain plasticity shows that we can actually create new neural pathways and alter the physical structure of our brains by thinking differently and changing our habits. Contrary to early scientific beliefs, the brain is not like a machine and neither is it *hardwired* like a computer. Neuroplasticity not only gives hope to those with mental challenges, but expands our understanding of the healthy brain and the resilience of human nature.

And this is great news for us.

As Norman Doidge writes in his book *The Brain That Changes Itself: Stories of Personal Triumph from the Frontiers of Brain Science*:

> The idea that the brain can change its own structure and function through thought and activity is, I believe, the most important alteration in our view of the brain since we first sketched out its basic anatomy and the workings of its basic component, the neuron . . . The neuroplastic revolution has implications for, among other things, our understanding of how love, sex, grief, relationships, learning, addictions, culture, technology, and psychotherapies change our brains.[5]

Without getting bogged down in the science, this means that adopting new cognitive techniques (or thinking skills) can not only improve our immediate life experience, but also alter the structure of our brains for more positive and *sustainable* life change.

Maybe it's time to view your brain as a muscle that can be strengthened with practice (just like your biceps).

I find it helpful to consider the analogy of working out at the gym. As I write, I'm sitting on my buns of steel (in the making) and I have to say I'm pretty sore. You see, yesterday was 'legs day' with my dynamic 22-year-old personal trainer, Jess. Although I'd had a month's break from training, Jess didn't let me slacken off – she drove me hard! I squatted, lifted, pushed and pulled my way through an hour of heavy weights and light banter. The entire focus of the session was on my glutes, lower back and legs. So, as you can imagine, those muscles are feeling tight, sore and rather uncomfortable today.

When we lift weights at the gym, the myofibrils within our muscle fibres are damaged. This damage triggers our muscles to start the repair process, rebuilding the microtears so the muscles become stronger.

Ouch! No wonder it hurts. We actually tear our muscles; we *consciously choose* to do some damage to our bodies. And WHY do we do this? Because we know it is a means to an end – a small amount of pain today leads to fantastic results down the track.

We exchange pain for pay-off.

So what if we apply this to our life outside the gym?

Let's say you have an unhelpful habit of speaking over others. You are an intelligent, vivacious woman who is full of ideas and energy, and when you have an idea you want to share it – immediately! Sometimes, this means you don't carefully listen to others and you often interrupt. As a result, you can come across as rude or abrasive, but you're not! You know you have loads of compassion and respect for other people, but your mouth just gets carried away sometimes. People have described you as having 'no filter' and you have noticed that colleagues often get defensive in response to your interruptions.

You decide to change this habit.

While it's a seemingly simple change to make, it's not easy. *Simple*, because you simply need to swap some words and behaviours for some others, but not *easy*, because you have developed a behavioural pattern that has been embedded and reinforced over years. You feel like this behaviour is part of you: 'I'm the one who butts in.'

As you start to work through the process of changing this behaviour (self-awareness, recognition of your patterns, learning to stop and swap, and integrating the new behaviour into your communication patterns), you face internal resistance. It's so uncomfortable! When in conversations, you feel incredibly frustrated because you know you have something relevant to say, but you hold yourself back. You want to speak over others when you disagree, but force yourself to wait for a natural pause in the conversation – you hate this! It feels unnatural, uncomfortable and wrong. AKA the pain.

But you persevere. Over time, you start to relax into this new way of communicating and, thanks to brain plasticity, your neural pathways adapt and you start to create a new way for your brain to function. The great news is that people start to respond differently to you – they smile and nod when you talk (rather than looking frustrated and defensive), ask for your input and actively engage you in discussions. You start to feel more valued, your self-esteem is boosted by their encouragement and you feel more connected to others. AKA the pay-off.

I applaud Doidge's work and find it incredibly inspiring that we, as human beings, have the capacity to change the structure and function of our own brains (if you haven't read his book, I highly recommend it). I also think it is critical that we are realistic about the process of changing our mindsets and approach the process with our eyes open. Many of the stories I'll share and techniques I'll teach you here in this book relate to *personal change*.

Personal change requires work. Sometimes it will require moving through an uncomfortable phase (pain) to get to the positive outcome you desire (pay-off).

But trust me, it's worth it.

TAKE A CLOSER LOOK AT YOUR MINDSET

Let me introduce you to another imaginary character, Jack. Jack is a 14-year-old boy with the nickname 'Ratbag'. He lives in a chaotic household with his mum who struggles with depression and his step-dad who is often aggressive. Jack's older brother (whom he idolises) is in jail for low-level drug crimes and Jack's mates think he's heading in the same direction. At school, he's often disruptive in class (if he turns up at all). His teachers describe him as 'not that bright'. Jack is excited by risk-taking and has been known to surf a train or two.

How would you define Jack?

- A – a loser who is destined for a life of crime. He'll drop out of school soon and will probably die young due to his poor choices and lack of impulse control.
- B – a kid with as much potential as the next. He has the opportunity to respond to positive role models and learn new ways to view himself, perceive his world and solve problems.

If you answered A, you are looking at Jack with a **fixed mindset**. According to Carol Dweck in her book *Mindset: Changing the Way You Think to Fulfil Your Potential*, this is the belief that ability is innate and unchangeable. A fixed mindset does not allow for the possibility that people can change, evolve or develop. This style of thinking often blocks or limits development.

If you answered B, you are looking at Jack with a **growth mindset**. According to Dweck, this is the belief that a person's capacities and talents can improve over time. This style of thinking often leads to self-improvement, a tendency to persevere in the face of challenges and the ability to see problems as opportunities.[6]

Sometimes, we have to reach a crisis point or have a wake-up call in life to become aware that our mindset has been fixed and needs to become more flexible and growth focused. More often than not, our mindset is set to autopilot and we go about our lives automatically reacting to people and situations without much deep consideration of the way we are doing it.

You could say, we don't always THINK about the way we THINK – this is called metacognition.

Let's pause here for a moment to think about metacognition (that would be meta-metacognition, wouldn't it?). It's an important process to be aware of and, by grasping this now, it will make your understanding of and practical application of this book much smoother. Metacognition is a self-regulation process that enables you to step outside of yourself and examine your thinking from a bird's-eye view, as if you're witnessing yourself from above. It's such a key skill to have and, I believe, something that can set you apart in life, because – I'll let you in on a little secret – most people don't do it. Most people don't take the time to stop and ask themselves, 'How am I thinking about this situation?'

Metacognition involves applying a critical eye to:

* your own thinking and learning style
* yourself as a thinker and learner.

Journal time

METACOGNITION MOMENT

Are you ready to apply some metacognition to yourself? It's time to think about your thinking.

Select an area of your life – education, career, dating, relationships, parenting, family, finance, body image, a hobby, travel – anything you'd like to examine.

Now, ask yourself these questions and record your answers in your journal:

* WHAT are some typical thoughts you have about this life area?
* Describe the QUALITY of these thoughts (for example, are they open, harsh, expansive, limiting, curious, closed?).
* When it comes to change or growth in this area, what do you TELL YOURSELF?
* Consider your MINDSET in this area – is it a GROWTH mindset or a FIXED mindset?

Take the time to reflect on what you wrote. Now that you have developed some deeper awareness of your thinking in this area of your life, get CRITICAL! How could you adapt or change your thinking to improve your life experience and satisfaction? Write your answer to this in your journal and let your ideas flow.

I've noticed something over the years about the typical behaviour of people with fixed versus growth mindsets:

- People with a fixed mindset tend to say NO.
- People with a growth mindset tend to say YES.

I'm sure you know someone who has a fixed mindset, or maybe you've had moments in your life when you've been stuck in a fixed state. It's quite easy to spot: it tends to be characterised by inflexibility and, you guessed it, underpinned by our old mate, FEAR.

SPOTLIGHT ON JANE | JUST SAY YES

I'd like to introduce you to my former client Jane (not her real name). Jane and I first met when she was in her late thirties and living a full, stimulating and fulfilling life.

As a busy doctor with her own practice, Jane invested heavily in her life and career; she took herself on regular holidays, had monthly massages and facials, ate healthy food and exercised regularly.

She was a woman who knew how to date herself.

But Jane had developed a negative habit, a mental pattern that had emerged over years of putting herself and her career first. Jane's default reply to anything that even resembled a social invitation was NO.

Being part of a wide and active social circle, Jane was regularly invited to all sorts of activities. From weekend hikes to relaxed brunches, from champagne sundowners to film festivals, she routinely knocked back all offers. This habit developed gradually over many years.

In her twenties she was typically studying or paying her dues as a junior doctor in the hospital system and social events were just not on her radar. As she drifted into her thirties and her busy practice took off, she disappeared from the social scene altogether.

Jane had made herself socially invisible. Not surprisingly, she had not had a date for a very, very long time.

We worked together on Jane's mindset. She had spent many years programming her brain to say NO in the name of self-protection and, unbeknown to her, self-sabotage.

It took a while for Jane to become consciously aware that this was her pattern but, when she did, it was like a giant neon heart-shaped light bulb began flashing above her head.

Now, 20 years of habitual behaviour is hard to change and it takes time. So Jane and I agreed on one small change: she would say YES to a social invitation *once* per week.

That's all. As simple as that.

At first, Jane found this annoying. She had built up a very independent life and was not accustomed to spontaneous social events interrupting her well-planned schedule. She felt quite conflicted about being true to her own commitments versus expanding her comfort zone and becoming a social being.

I assisted her to sit with her Free Floating Anxiety (for Jane, this was a generalised feeling of anxiety about making changes in her life) and start to find acceptance in the idea that change could be positive for her.

As the weeks progressed, each YES became a little easier. She started small – a one-hour coffee here, a 45-minute beach walk there. After a couple of months, Jane started looking forward to the next invitation and, in fact, started initiating social connections with her friends. She was starting to awaken her own playful and relaxed side (a side that had been asleep for a long time).

So, at around the 12-week mark, Jane was totally relaxed when her friend invited her to a gathering of people from a totally new social group. In the past, she would not have even considered attending, but her confidence had increased over the past few months; she had enjoyed some great conversations with new people and she found herself bubbling with anticipation about the new social arena.

It was a relaxed barbecue at a friend of a friend's home. Jane eased into the new environment and gently connected with a range of people from different backgrounds. She loved the feeling of excitement she felt before meeting each new person, the anticipation of what was to come.

When Jane met Raj, another doctor, she naturally fell into a comfortable conversation, talking shop. Although they had medicine in common, they lived very different lives. Where Jane had built a safe cocoon for herself and stuck to a rather strict life routine, Raj worked all over the world and enjoyed a spontaneous, adventurous lifestyle.

She was drawn to his openness and courage – traits that she knew she had but ones that were hidden deep inside her.

Their conversation developed and Jane found herself becoming attracted to Raj.

**Now that she was in her new zone of YES,
Jane took a risk.**

She suggested that they catch up for a drink sometime after the barbecue and Raj agreed.

Jane and Raj started dating and spent the next few months stealing moments whenever they could. Jane really enjoyed the feeling of opening up and letting him in. She still felt a twinge of discomfort each time she changed her routine to see him, but she persisted and enjoyed the ride.

Raj was involved in a number of international projects so before long they found themselves in a long-distance relationship. After a while, Jane realised that she wanted more.

Having been through such a journey of self-awakening and arriving at the point where she believed she was ready for love, she didn't want a part-time lover.

She ended it with Raj on good terms and stepped into a more proactive social and dating life, ready to meet her next big love.

Last time we spoke, Jane was enjoying casually dating a few guys and taking her time to find the right person for her. She had cut back on her hours in her practice, had hired an assistant and was starting to live a more balanced life.

And all this eventuated by just saying YES.

Journal time

SAY YES

Take some time to reflect on each of your life areas. Are there any parts of your life where you feel a little stuck? Perhaps you've settled into an unhelpful pattern or developed an overly rigid way of living in this part of your life. I wonder if you've unconsciously created a pattern of saying NO somewhere in your life.

Select a life area and ask yourself:

- What do I currently say NO to in this life area?
- What does saying NO deprive me of?
- How does this make me feel?
- What could I start saying YES to in this area of my life?
- How would this change my experience?
- How would this make me feel?
- What would this mean to me?
- What is currently stopping me from saying YES? How can I overcome this?

- How motivated am I to change my experience in this area of my life?

Feel free to apply these questions to as many life areas as are relevant for you. Remember to be kind and self-compassionate as you do this – it's not about judging yourself for saying NO, it's about exploring the possibilities when you say YES.

YOU ARE NOT YOUR FEAR

One thing I need you to understand is that *you are not your emotions*. You are a separate entity from your emotional life – it doesn't own you.

Try to imagine an **emotional bubble** that floats gently next to you, everywhere you go. All of your emotions (both helpful and unhelpful ones) live inside here – they accompany you but do not live inside you.

When you experience any emotion – let's say fear – you can look to the bubble to remind yourself that it is separate from you. You can choose to either:

- pop the bubble and absorb yourself in the seductive, squishy, slippery, confusing mess, or
- look at the bubble, examine it, understand it, accept it and move on with an understanding of what role this emotion plays in your life (this is the less messy option!).

Use your language to reinforce this approach, for example:

BEING YOUR EMOTION	OBSERVING YOUR EMOTION
I am scared.	I feel scared about . . .
I am stupid.	I did a stupid thing that made me feel . . .
I am anxious.	This situation is making me feel anxious so I am going to . . .

BE AGILE

Susan David is the renowned Harvard psychologist who c
term **emotional agility**.[7] In her research into emotions, happiness
and achievement, she looked at the difference between people who
were slaves to their emotions and people who could be flexible and
adaptable with their emotions, those who could separate themselves
from their emotional bubble and use their emotions to propel them
towards their goals.

She found that, while emotionally agile people are not immune to
stress and fear (it's not a cure for bad-hair days), the key difference is
that they know how to adapt, aligning their actions with their values and
making small but powerful changes that lead to a lifetime of growth.
According to David, emotional agility is not about ignoring difficult
emotions and thoughts, it's about *holding them loosely,* facing them
courageously and compassionately, and then moving past them to
bring the best of yourself forward.

I really like David's approach because it's not about pretending the
unhelpful feelings don't exist – you know they are there! This is not
about denial; it's about acceptance and being smart about the choices
you make in response to your feelings. It's also about understanding
that you are *not* your fear, you are *not* your emotions.

I'd like you to keep her concept of holding your emotions loosely front
of mind as you progress through this book. Remember to maintain a
growth mindset (start by saying YES) and believe you have the capacity
to change and transform – *because you do.* Keep in mind that you are
not your fear and remember that Imposter Syndrome can be combated
with a sweet little recognition fantasy. You are on your way to mastering
your fear – the first step in the C Word Method and the foundation
of your confidence journey.

FEAR
MASTERY

CHAPTER 3

THROUGH
their
EYES

This chapter addresses issues of bullying, racism, body shaming, sexual assault and gender questioning. If any of these issues are a little too close to your experience and you'd rather not place your focus here, please move on to the next chapter.

•

By now, you might be thinking to yourself, 'Sure, it's fine for other women to overcome fear and find their confidence but what about me? I have [insert major life obstacle of your choice] to deal with.'

You may even look at ME and think, 'You're an educated, middle-class, cis-gendered, straight white woman living in the developed world. Why wouldn't you be confident?'

And you'd be right.

Let me check my privilege right here. Other than typical white-girl problems, I haven't really had to overcome any major obstacles on my journey to confidence. Apart from being a woman, and therefore a member of a marginalised group, I've had a pretty smooth road. Yes, I've faced the grief of miscarriage like so many women and, just like you, I'm devastated by the epidemic of violence against women. I've grappled with the gender pay-gap and have personal experience of being paid significantly less than a male counterpart, and I'm frustrated by the underrepresentation of women in leadership.

But I am also hyper-aware that, in addition to being a woman, you may also belong to another marginalised group that means society constantly conspires against your self-efficacy and self-worth.

My experience as a psychologist, and as a human, tells me that many women endure a daily battle with dark forces that undermine their confidence.

This is valid and real and not to be minimised.

Globally, in addition to sexism and misogyny, women have to deal with many other unconscious biases that exist in our society. These are underlying attitudes and prejudices about who a woman is and what she is capable of based on her:

- ethnicity
- sexual orientation
- gender diversity
- trauma experience
- disability
- body size and shape
- socioeconomic status.

Do these factors impact your willingness and ability to take bold action? Damn right they do.

Should they stand in your way of becoming a confident woman?

No. They should not.

Now, I know that I am in no position to talk to you about experience as a marginalised woman. So I've turned to three people with lived experience in some of these areas – they have their own stories, their own voices, and have generously agreed to share them with you.

Now that's brave.

POINTING THE FINGER WITHIN

Before we meet our guests, let's take a look within.

So far in this book, we've spent some time together, exploring fear. By now, you have probably started to reflect on the things in your life that trigger a fear response, considered your own physical and behavioural signs of fear and started to contemplate how you can live 'alongside' fear on your journey to confidence. No doubt you are starting to get the picture that a big part of mastering fear is your mindset.

Self-talk is generally derived from two sources: those internal to you (based on your innate beliefs, values and views on the world) and those external to you (social influences, world events, cultural biases and prejudices). Our self-talk is based on the stories that we internalise and make our own.

Sometimes, we internalise stories that are cruel and judgmental and do not serve us; internalised misogyny, racism, homophobia or transphobia, for example, can form the basis of an internal critic.

It's not unusual for the external world, in all its messy, problematic glory, to seep into our subconscious world and start telling us stories about ourselves that undermine our self-esteem, self-worth and confidence.

Now, this might sound counterintuitive and, in many ways, it is, because:

- Why would a woman 'hate' women?
- Why would a person of colour 'hate' people of different ethnic backgrounds?
- Why would a gay person 'hate' people in the LGBTQIA+ community?

It's not logical or rational, and often occurs purely at the unconscious level. You may have come across the term 'unconscious bias' – well, the above situations show a form of unconscious bias directed inward. It's a belief in negative stereotypes about a group that YOU belong to, therefore you're believing that also about yourself. Biases are mental shortcuts, rather cognitively lazy ways of making quick judgments. When it comes to making self-assessments, it's often quicker to ignore the nuance and go for the stereotype.

For example, as a woman:

THE STEREOTYPE	THE NUANCE
I am a woman and women are bitchy, therefore I am bitchy.	I have complex relationships with my girlfriends. Sometimes I feel jealous of them, sometimes I judge their choices, sometimes I wonder why we are even friends. Sometimes I lose my temper with them, especially when they press my hot buttons.
I am a woman and women are ditsy and scattered, therefore I am ditsy and scattered.	I often carry a million things in my mind at once. I'm juggling emotional relationships, complex group dynamics, my own feelings, my thoughts about what I'm doing tomorrow and what I did yesterday, my focus on the task at hand, and dreams about what I'd rather be doing.

As you can clearly see here, overlooking the nuance and going straight for the stereotype is reductive and unfair on yourself. It is an over-simplification of who you are and a sure-fire way to undermine your own confidence.

I have to say, I've noticed myself doing this. There is a stereotype out there about professional people who appear on reality TV – they are 'sell-outs', fake experts, who are just there for entertainment purposes and add no real value. This belief is often heavily reinforced through social media. Now, although I have spent 20 years as a psychologist and have loads of experience in counselling, advising and coaching people, there have been times when I have internalised this stereotype. I have wondered, 'Do I really have what it takes? Am I a fake?' Fortunately, I have rational and supportive people around me who help me stay grounded (thanks, Hubby) and keep me focused on my strengths – sometimes I really need to be reminded.

Sometimes, I believe the bad press.

So, take a moment now to pause and reflect on this. Do you sometimes believe your own bad press?

Journal time

MY INTERNALISED BIAS

Do you belong to a marginalised group or groups?

What are the common stereotypes attributed to this group or these groups?

Be really honest with yourself now. Have you unwittingly taken on any of these stereotypes and adopted them as your own self-talk? Have you ever caught yourself saying things to yourself, based on these unfair stereotypes?

Create two columns in your journal under the headings:
- The stereotype
- The nuance

Spend some time fleshing out your own nuances. Fill in the colour, the detail, that the stereotype overlooks.

Now create two more columns with the headings:
- The stereotypical self-talk
- The nuanced self-talk

This is your opportunity to reframe any self-talk that has been corrupted by unfair stereotypes and make it your own. Make your self-talk compassionate, nurturing and uplifting.

THREE UNIQUE VOICES

It's time to introduce you to my three guests. These are the three individuals I have asked to talk to you about their journey to confidence: two women and one man.

Yep, a man.

So let me tell you a bit about our three guests.

MEET KAYA

Kaya Wilson is a writer and tsunami scientist based in Australia. He was the winner of the 2019 Writing NSW Varuna Fellowship, a runner-up in the 2019 *Kill Your Darlings* New Critic Award and shortlisted for Penguin Australia's 2019 Write It Fellowship. His first book, *As Beautiful as Any Other: A Memoir of My Body*, was published in 2021.

Kaya is also a transgender man.

Having transitioned in his thirties, Kaya is in the unique position of having lived experience presenting as a girl, a female teenager, a young woman *and* a man. He has experienced the social impact of being a 'masculine presenting' female, a person going through transition and, now, a man constantly wondering if he is 'passing' as a man in the world. And, critically, Kaya has felt what it feels like to be a female *as well as* a male when it comes to the experience and manifestation of confidence. My key question to explore with Kaya was, 'How does the development of confidence differ when presenting as a female versus a male?'

MEET CASEY

When I say 'meet' Casey, I say it in a very loose way as you probably already feel like you know Casey Donovan. In 2004, at the age of just 16, Casey became the youngest ever winner of *Australian Idol*. Over the last 17 years, she has received acclaim as a musician as well as an actor, presenter and author. She has been nominated for – and won – multiple awards, including an ARIA No. 1 Award for 'Listen with Your Heart' and Deadly Awards for Best Album, Best Single and Most Promising New Talent.

Casey is an Indigenous Australian, a Gumbaynggirr and Dungari woman, and identifies as a lesbian and a plus-size woman. I was interested to explore her experience of standing on stage (perhaps one of the most exposing and vulnerable things a person can do) and finding her confidence while simultaneously battling discrimination based on her background and size. With Casey, I wondered, 'How does she quieten the external criticism to focus on her very high profile profession?'

MEET SIMONNE

Full disclosure here: Simonne Michelle is a close friend of mine. She is a senior leader at Beyond Blue and a feminist writer who speaks, writes and teaches about shame, trauma and intimacy, and about how to unearth our true authenticity.

Simonne (AKA Mon) also happens to be a survivor of childhood and adult sexual abuse, which began when she was four. Over the years, we have shared many a coffee and discussed the details of her history, but, until now, we hadn't unpacked what it took to process and work through trauma on her pathway to authentic confidence. With Mon, I wondered, 'What was the turning point or "thing" that enabled her to put her trauma to the side and allow her confidence to blossom?'

WHEN FEAR SHOWS UP

Each of my three guests face daily prejudice and pressure based on either a personal characteristic or something that happened to them. For each, a unique combination of fears and unconscious biases exists beneath the surface, informing and influencing their daily lives.

For Casey, the very nature of her job involves stepping onto a stage or in front of a camera, which can be an incredibly vulnerable space for even the most confident of us. Her fears of judgment and **rejection** are ever-present when she puts herself out there: 'I'm big and this still plays into my mind with my confidence . . . I feel like I can't do things because of my size. So therefore I don't try.' When I asked where she thinks some of her negative self-talk comes from, Casey shared, 'I think it comes from a place of rejection. Like being told I cannot. So because I physically know I can't, I'm not going to go up and say, well, I'd like to do this please, and then they say, sorry, you can't because of your weight, and I'd be like, oh no!'

Casey is incredibly self-aware and seems to fully grasp the impact of her body size and background on her career mindset. As a lighter skinned Indigenous woman, she is sometimes thought to be Greek or Italian, which can broaden the scope of the roles she is considered for, but it can also work against her: 'Sometimes I'm not black enough, I don't look Indigenous enough and therefore I don't get roles.' For Casey, the fear of rejection based on her body size or background is a very real factor in her career, and therefore is impossible to avoid. She can't avoid the rejection – it's part of the job – but she can change the way she *experiences* this rejection.

For Simonne, her early experience of sexual assault taught her to avoid being **vulnerable**. She learned from a tender age that opening herself up to people, especially men, was an unsafe proposition to be avoided at all costs. As she says, 'It made me very promiscuous . . . I became promiscuous in my late teens. The reason why is that I sought love, affection, safety and security in a place that felt weirdly comfortable . . . sort of inappropriate sexual experiences. And so I sought love from men, particularly older men. And I had no confidence in myself other than as a sexual being for men. So my identity was wrapped up in what I looked like and what I represented to the people around me, and I only saw men.'

For Mon, this fear of vulnerability led to her detaching from her romantic relationships, essentially just going through the motions: 'I had really strong memories at university of just being laser-focused on relationships and men and sex. And I didn't enjoy any of it. So it was a very lonely existence because I didn't really form a relationship with myself. There was a deep relationship outside of what I saw my worth as and I saw my worth as purely a sexual being.' She took a job as a stripper and exotic dancer where she 'performed confidence' and 'looked confident' and 'there was a distinct comfort in the discomfort . . . but I didn't feel sexy, just terrified'.

Kaya's early life experience, presenting as a girl on a scholarship at a highbrow English boarding school, was fraught with contradictions. While he was highly driven to achieve academically and incredibly focused on leadership pursuits, he was also afraid of **humiliation** and **exposure**. Although he didn't self-identify as a teen questioning his gender identity, he knew he was different: 'I hated shaving my legs and I would wear navy tights thinking, oh they can't see. But then I found out some boys were calling me Chewbacca [the hairy Wookiee warrior who appeared in the *Star Wars* movies] behind my back . . . that was one way that I kind of protected myself, not shaving my legs. It would always get kind of exposed, picked up.'

For all our guests, living with the fear of rejection, vulnerability, humiliation and exposure (among other things) was incredibly stressful and emotionally draining. For Kaya and Simonne, particularly, who lived with these fears as children and adolescents, it's highly likely that these heavy burdens had an impact on their social, emotional and intellectual development.

THE IMPOSTER

In the last chapter you'll remember that we looked at Imposter Syndrome and discovered that, in many cases, what sits beneath this mindset is FEAR. Some of the common fears underlying Imposter Syndrome include fear of:

- being less than perfect
- social or intimate rejection
- abandonment
- humiliation

- vulnerability
- success.

Now that you're getting to know our three guests, you can see how some of these fears may be manifesting for them. Not surprisingly, I didn't need to mention the concept of Imposter Syndrome during our interviews; they were all well aware of its presence and impact.

According to Casey, 'There's still this fear and then the Imposter Syndrome comes in because you're like, well, I wasn't made for this role. Can I do this role? And then those conversations start happening. Am I able to do that? Will they allow me to do things differently?'

Imagine the impact of standing in front of a panel of entertainment industry professionals, totally raw and exposed as you audition, with questions like these running through your mind. Can you imagine what this mindset would do to your performance? Not likely to bring out your best, yet Casey still finds it within herself to shine.

Simonne believes that Imposter Syndrome started interrupting her confidence when she was very young. A talented writer, she would submit writing and win awards, but constantly questioned whether she was actually competent or deserving. This shows up for her today as an adult in a high-powered executive career, where she feels like a 'girl' rather than a 'woman'. We've had many conversations over the years where she says things like, 'They have no idea I don't know what I'm doing . . . it's only a matter of time until they figure it out' (AKA textbook Imposter Syndrome manifestation). In her highly accomplished career, Mon plays down her achievements and dwells on her skill gaps, all the while being highly self-aware and attuned to the magnitude of the situation. In her words: 'I think the Imposter Syndrome is based in really old stuff. Shame-based stuff. Shame has interfered with how I see myself and how I think the world sees me.'

For many of us, Imposter Syndrome is one of the frustrating, but common ways fear shows up in our lives.

FEAR FATIGUE

As I'm sure you've experienced in your life, another common reaction to and consequence of fear is **anxiety** (see Chapter 5, p. 101, for more on anxiety). In fact, many people describe fear and anxiety as almost intertwined, and it can be tricky to identify the difference between the two. But typically, anxiety is experienced as an emotional and behavioural reaction to a perceived fear or threat.

If you've ever experienced fear and anxiety for an extended period of time, you'll know that it can be overwhelmingly draining. Casey described her experience of fear fatigue: 'I think I just get to the point where my anxiety starts to burn me out, as well as jobs and saying yes to everything. It's that feeling of constant anxiety, just being tired and starting to just emotionally remove from the situation. I notice when my burnout's coming. I start looking at emotion and I'm triple-guessing myself in that moment instead of just going through it. It's hard.'

It's easy to imagine how draining this would be, especially the double- and triple-checking all thoughts and decisions. With this type of constant fear and anxiety, there seems to be no 'off button', it's just ever-present and overloads your cognitive, emotional and mental resources.

Kaya recalls experiencing fear fatigue presenting as a girl in the boarding school environment: 'I felt like this a lot. And then what would happen is I would be spinning all these plates and then, every six or seven weeks . . . I'd get sick. I'd collapse and then start again; it was very cyclical. And the school clinic staff knew me and they just put me straight to bed. I just slept there for two days, from exhaustion.' I asked Kaya if some of this fear-anxiety-exhaustion cycle was related to essentially wearing a mask, pretending to be someone he was not, day in and day out. He replied, 'Yeah . . . I could only sustain it and then . . . it just happened over and over.'

I wonder if you have ever experienced this cycle? Sometimes, living with fear can make you feel like a mouse running on a never-ending wheel – constant, enduring, unwavering pressure that either overtly or insidiously wears you down. And if you don't do anything to break the cycle, you step straight back onto that wheel again.

Exhausting.

STEPPING INTO COURAGE

**Remember: Courage emerges when what you
want is stronger than what you fear.**

One of the reasons I chose these three particular people for my interviews was their demonstrated capacity to not just live alongside fear, but also challenge and overcome it. This doesn't mean that fear is no longer present in their lives; it means that they all have the emotional maturity, self-awareness and sheer GUTS to live extraordinary lives in spite of it.

We can't change our histories but we can change the stories we tell ourselves about our histories. We can challenge and reframe the fears when they emerge, and we can choose to take courageous action in the direction of our goals.

Being **goal-directed** might be described as one of the antidotes to living a life of fear. When we have clear, specific, measurable goals, our desires come into clear focus. When we know what we want, and WHY it's important to us, our fears start to become less of a main character in our stories.

Knowing your WHY can help quieten the voice of fear.

For Simonne, her WHY became extremely clear as she got older: she wanted to be a mother. Through her thirties, this became her number one goal and priority in life. When she encountered fertility issues, she took courageous action in the form of IVF – six cycles! (I personally went through just one cycle and even that took an incredible toll on my mind and body; I can't imagine what this process was like for her.)

KNOWING YOUR *WHY*
can help
quieten the
VOICE
OF FEAR.

When she found herself with a young child in an 11-year marriage where the latter six years were completely void of intimacy, Mon had a tough decision to make. Would she stay or leave? Unconsciously, she was likely weighing up her fear of being alone versus the strength of her love for her daughter. As she explains it:

> My daughter was two at that point, two and a half – was this what I wanted her to see? What I wanted for her? What do I want her vision of intimacy to be and what will she grow up seeing? Because this will form her view of intimate relationships. And it kind of struck me that what she was seeing was not an intimate relationship at all – we might have held hands but there was no passion and no intimacy. She just saw two best friends having a great time together, because we did – we're like brother and sister. Because ultimately, due to the sexual abuse in my past, I had married a version of my father to try and feel safe and protected, but, as a consequence, we had no sexual intimacy at all. But I thought, that's going to be what she thinks intimacy is. Is that what I want for her?

Simonne's WHY, her love for her little girl, was stronger than her fear of leaving her marriage. So she did it (and you can read more about her life in her book *Shame and the Hero*).

Kaya made perhaps one of the most complicated decisions a human can make, to transition from one gender to another. The complexity of this decision cannot be overstated (and if you'd like to learn more about his transition experience, read his memoir *As Beautiful As Any Other*). Kaya's WHY was possibly present from a very young age, but became consciously available later in life. As a child and teen, Kaya felt different from other kids and knew there was something missing, but perhaps found it difficult to identify or label what it was. By the time they reached adulthood, had defined their bisexuality and built a solid support network in the queer community, Kaya was in a position to embrace their WHY. They wanted to be their authentic self.

Kaya's desire to be himself (the WHY) was stronger than the fear of rejection, humiliation or exposure (the FEAR).

Casey is a storyteller, a performer, an entertainer. It might seem illogical to you that she experiences performance anxiety and self-doubt, yet still chooses to step on stage. You might find it hard to believe that she would have the mortifying experience of becoming 'frozen' on stage or forgetting her lines in front of a live audience, then still choose to turn up the next day and step on that same stage again. Surely it would be easier to take a different career direction? Not for Casey – she is living her WHY every day. She wakes up and actively chooses to be a performer because this is who she is, this is her identity.

Casey's WHY (her strong desire to live the life of a professional performer) is stronger than her performance anxiety or self-critical internal monologue telling her she can't do it.

So, over to you. What is your WHY? What is your greatest FEAR? Which one is stronger?

Journal time

MY WHY VERSUS MY FEAR

For this activity, I'd suggest a less structured approach. You're delving into your subconscious mind to get to the core of your motivation and drive – what is it that is most important to you? And what are you most afraid of?

So, I recommend you spend some time writing in a 'stream of consciousness' or 'free association' style – no rules, no editing, no judgment – just write. Let it flow, try not to overthink it, just write.

Enjoy the process and, once you've finished, leave it for a week and then return to it. What insights do you notice?

PERFORMATIVE CONFIDENCE

One of the most interesting insights to come out of these three interviews was the consistent reference to what I call performative confidence. You might call it false confidence or 'faking it', but I see it as a step on the road to authentic confidence. It reminds me of a little girl attempting to walk in her mother's stilettos – it's awkward and unnatural, and not very effective, but it helps her feel more prepared if one day she chooses to wear the real thing. Simonne found herself performing a version of confidence when she took to the stage as a stripper:

> I didn't know how to move my body in a sexual way because there was terror. I only experienced sex as fear-based and yet I still went down that road. So, yes, that was a [type of] confidence; the confidence was because I knew that men wanted me, because they always had; like I said, I couldn't ever remember them not. So there was a confidence in knowing that I was able to do it and that's what I'm here to do. And so I became a not very good exotic dancer and stripper and I looked confident and I had long blonde hair like a Barbie doll and I knew what to do and I knew how to speak and all of that.

When Kaya was a teen, he felt like he was playing the role of a girl, 'but it was a bit of a veneer, you know?' Kaya was school captain, involved in team sports and engaged in all the things that a confident girl *should* be seen to be doing: 'Yes, I had boyfriends, but I think they'd feel like an act. A lot of it.' It would seem that Kaya's experience of confidence presenting as a girl may not have been deeply rooted in their identity, but rather another skill to demonstrate to the outside world.

For Casey, stepping into a role and literally pretending to be someone else on stage can be a very comforting thing: 'That's what's great about playing a character. It's like, well, this is your character's time now, Casey has to just wait, which is nice to be able to do that.'

She talked about her experience of playing the formidable role of Mama Morton in the musical *Chicago*. The Morton character has a booming presence on stage and Casey had to get up on stage every night to deliver this uber-confidence. Some days, Casey might have had a bad day, eaten food she regretted or not looked after herself, but she still had to step into the Mama Morton character and *act confident*. For the most part, she said she was able to detach from her own emotions and absorb herself in the role (a therapeutic process in itself), but sometimes her own self-doubts would come through in Morton's mannerisms, perhaps softening the character's impact.

SIMPLE STRATEGIES

I learned so much from each of my guests and have so much admiration for their courage and resilience. If I had to choose one simple lesson to share with you from each person, it would be:

- When Simonne's Imposter Syndrome shows up and she feels like a girl in women's clothing at work, she pulls out a photo of herself at 12 years of age because, as she describes it, 'The person who turns up to work is a girl. And that's a very recent realisation, and there are great things I can do now about that. I can put a photo of me at 12 over there and say, you're going to sit over there while the adult is going to sit in the chair and work.' This is a great visual cue and reality-checking device, keeping her grounded in reality and separating her past from her present.
- When Kaya transitioned and had to 'come out' every time he encountered someone who knew him pre-transition, he relied on a handy script: 'You sort of develop a sentence – you say, "Oh, I'm transgender. I'm a guy now."' This was a highly effective way to simplify a complex message and take the pressure off during potentially emotionally charged situations.

- And when Casey experiences stage fright, AKA performance anxiety, she uses a deflection and deferral strategy. She reflected, 'I think you physically have to tell yourself, you can't do this now you're working, come back in an hour and we'll deal with it then, because you have to be on the ball and on point.' This is not to be confused with avoidance; Casey is not putting off the fear-based thoughts altogether, just deferring them until a later time when she'll have the headspace to deal with them.

So, we have a visual device, a script and a deferral strategy. These are all simple yet highly effective strategies for helping you step out of fear and into courage.

Which ones will you use?

part
two

Smart Courage

FEAR
MASTERY

SMART
COURAGE

DEEP
CONFIDENCE

FLUID
COMPETENCE

> Courage is resistance to fear,
> mastery of fear, not absence of fear.
>
> **MARK TWAIN**

Smart Courage is about learning to live alongside fear in a bold and empowered way.

Now that you have started to understand your own fear response, discovered tools to help you master the role of fear in your life and observed some great examples of how managing fear can enable progress, you are ready to examine courage.

Smart, courageous behaviour is activated when you can manage fear and think strategically about what you want – and you can do this in an emotionally considered manner. I'm going to show you how to expand your comfort zone, rather than stepping into the anxiety zone, and help you discover how you can introduce Smart Courage into your life.

You'll come to realise that taking smart, courageous action is the *only* way to get what you want and to live a truly extraordinary life.

SMART
COURAGE

CHAPTER 4

Smart

COURAGE

THE THINKING WOMAN'S SUIT OF ARMOUR

Okay, let's get something clear right from the start. Courage is not about fearlessness.

Courage is the way we respond to fear, the way we frame our fear and choose to behave in its face. You won't see me wearing a 'No Fear' T-shirt anytime soon – I believe fear is an important component of the confidence journey. To be courageous means you can act *in spite of* fear. Fear reminds us that we are alive, we have a past, our environment has an impact on us and we have challenges to overcome. And that's great!

The reason I'm taking you on a deep dive into courage right now is that courage is the gateway drug to confidence.

Time and time again, life experience shows us that by doing courageous things, and proving to ourselves that we *can* do them, we become more confident. Being courageous also offers a range of side-effects that add bonus points to your quality of life:

- Being courageous enables you to see the world from a range of different perspectives (that is, you look beyond your comfortable home-base).
- It makes you a more well-rounded person and expands your experience in life (AKA it makes you less boring).
- Being courageous typically leads to greater success in life because you're more likely to say YES and embrace opportunities as they arise.
- It increases your sense of accomplishment and happiness.
- Being courageous is contagious – when others observe your behaviour and the benefits it gives you, they start following suit.

Courageous thought and behaviour tend to have a snowball effect. To be honest, it can even become a little addictive. When you make the *small* decision to expand your comfort zone and try something new, step into *somewhat* unfamiliar territory, take a *calculated* risk and get a positive result, you experience a rush of POSITIVITY.

I'll pause here for a moment to point something out. Notice in the previous paragraph I used the words 'small', 'somewhat' and 'calculated'. I'm not being tentative, I'm intentionally pointing out that you don't have to take a giant leap into the unknown to be courageous – you can do it gradually, calmly and safely. More on this a bit later.

So let's explore courage together. We're going to look at how courage is defined for us as women, how we apply it in our lives and, importantly, how we can take the reins to lead ourselves through courage and into confidence.

GENDER DIFFERENCES IN COURAGE

I'll bet you're already familiar with this statistic:

Men apply for a job when they meet only 60 per cent of the qualifications, but women apply only if they meet 100 per cent of them.[8]

Why is it that men can take that 60 per cent of evidence-based results and extrapolate it to mean 'I can do it'? And, more importantly, why *can't* women take that 60–99 per cent of evidence-based results to make the same proclamation?

Think about this for a moment.

A man looks at a problem and knows that he only has 60 per cent of the tools he needs to solve that problem. He draws on everything he has been taught about males in our society, checks in with his self-belief and tells himself, 'Hell yes, I can do this!'

A woman looks at the same problem and knows that she has 60–99 per cent of the tools she needs to solve the problem. She draws on everything she has been taught about females in our society, checks in with her self-belief and tells herself, 'There is no way in hell I can do this!'

There is something in the socialisation of children in western society that expects boys to not only solve problems, but also back themselves to take risks and be successful. There is also something in the social fabric that expects girls to doubt their own capability, to avoid risks and to defer to others when it comes to solving problems.

There is clearly a *courage gap* that sits beside the *pay gap* and other gender-based gaps in our society. Sure, there are myriad cultural, environmental, social and political influences at play that may be beyond our control, but, as women, let's focus on what we *can* control – the way we choose to internalise social perceptions of women, to view ourselves and to take subsequent action.

Whether we are consciously aware of it or not, all of us have been influenced by our socialisation and the inherent message that 'boys are more competent than girls'.

Remember Kaya from Chapter 3? He is in a unique position to comment on this difference, given he has had the opportunity to present in the social and professional environment as a woman, then later as a man. Interestingly, Kaya even has the experience of showing up in the *same* workplace and meeting with the *same* people, pre- and post-transition.

Kaya related examples of speaking up in meetings when presenting as a woman and the experience of 'everyone ignoring it . . . like you're taking up too much space'. When they presented as a woman, Kaya recalls feeling that there was not an assumed level of their credibility and competence, they were constantly having to prove it.

Post-transition, Kaya said 'that stuff just changed almost overnight'.

He shared the story of a senior man he would regularly meet with, in the presence of a group of colleagues. When presenting as a woman, Kaya would speak up in the meetings and the senior man would avoid eye contact, directing most of his communication to the men in the room. These days, as a man, Kaya speaks up in the same forums, in the presence of most of the same people, and the senior man holds his eye contact and reinforces his ideas.

Kaya tried to make sense of this. He shared a surfing analogy by way of explanation: as a woman, you get one chance and if you miss out on the first wave, 'you don't get another wave'; whereas, as a man, your first wave is just the beginning of the process.

Essentially, as a man you are *allowed* to fail.

For someone who has been through such brutal discrimination and blatant inequality, Kaya is philosophical about it all. He is able to put it in perspective and tries to understand the behaviour of the senior man in his workplace as a response to unconscious conditioning. I found Kaya's empathy incredibly inspiring.

So, what can we take from Kaya's experience within the flawed social context of gendered expectations?

I think we can all borrow a leaf from Kaya's empathy book, in the first instance. Kaya teaches us that other people, in this case men, cannot necessarily help the systemic social lessons they have been dealt. In the most part, we can't change them and this is not the smartest place to focus our energy.

What we can change is ourselves.

We can look at the assumed 40 per cent gap in our knowledge or capacity and *choose* to have a go anyway. We can acknowledge the social expectations about speaking up and asking for our needs to be met, and do it anyway. We can discover that a situation or a choice involves a risk and a leap into the unknown, and we can leap anyway.

I'm talking about stepping into our potential as courageous women. Being courageous requires self-awareness, intelligence, empathy and the willingness to see the 40 per cent gap . . . and jump.

Journal time

BRIDGING THE 40 PER CENT GAP

Consider an area of your life where you believe that you only fulfil around 60 per cent of the required competence – for example:

- a career goal
- an artistic pursuit
- a practical skill
- sport or fitness
- a financial goal.

Now focus on that 40 per cent gap and try to define it:

- Is it really as big as 40 per cent? Is this realistic?
- Would other people see it the same way? (Ask them.)
- What are the features of this capability gap? What are you 'missing'?
- If you were a male, would you see this gap the same way?
- What do you believe is stopping you from taking the next step towards this goal?
- If you didn't know about the 40 per cent gap, what first step would you take towards this goal?
- What would be the next two steps?
- How would it feel to start bridging the gap and move towards your goal?
- How important is this to you?

TOXIC FEMININITY – HOW DO I SHAME THEE? LET ME COUNT THE WAYS

Before we delve into the deeper nature of female courage, let's take a moment to consider what it is NOT. To truly understand what it means to be a mature, well-adjusted, confident woman, it helps to examine the other side of the coin. Sadly, we see examples of female relationships taking a toxic turn too often in everyday life. Some women may mistakenly label these types of behaviours as 'courageous' but, in fact, they are simply examples of bullying.

Consider if you have ever encountered any of these situations with other women:

- being told you're showing too much skin
- being judged for choosing domestic duties *or* work outside the home
- hearing that you only received that promotion because you 'slept your way to the top'
- having another woman 'steal' your partner
- being rejected and judged for your sexual orientation or gender expression
- being shamed for not having children
- being shamed for your choices about birthing, feeding, sleeping or rearing your children
- being judged for owning your status as 'survivor'
- being cut down as part of the tall poppy syndrome
- being told you're not enough of, or too much of, a feminist
- feeling rejected due to your skin colour, ability or social status
- being told you're 'using your sexuality to your advantage'
- receiving side-eye and feeling another woman's judgmental gaze on your body
- being told your body size/shape is inappropriate for certain fashion styles
- hearing the opinion that you're 'punching above your weight' with your partner
- being disregarded as boring/insignificant/dull before you've had the chance to show your real self
- knowing that other women disapprove of your cosmetic surgery choices
- being made to feel 'less than' when other women perform moral superiority in relation to their ecological choices, food avoidances, weight management, fitness regimes, workaholism, alcohol or

caffeine restraint, competitive self-care or holistic approach to medicine (AKA virtue signalling).

You might call these feminine micro-aggressions or 'mean girl' behaviour. They are examples of the sisterhood turning against itself – while subtle to the outside observer, we all know that they cut deep and have long-lasting repercussions.

This is not courage.

I'm a firm believer in the sisterhood and I regularly use my network and expertise to actively support women. But I'm also aware that in our intimate female friendships we can sometimes walk a fine line between 'honest feedback', or as some say 'speaking my truth', and being downright cruel. You might notice examples of this when you watch reality TV, drama series or movies where some women justify their blatantly nasty behaviour against other women (kissing another woman's partner or publicly sharing her secrets, for example) by exclaiming, 'I was just being honest!'

This doesn't cut it.

As women, we have faced (and continue to face) enough persecution from outside the sisterhood that, surely, we deserve to feel safe within the sanctuary of our own feminine fold. Isn't it time that we stopped judging, blaming and shaming each other and started embracing our differences and enjoying everything we each have to offer?

So, what do all of the behaviours above have in common? If I were a betting woman, I'd suggest they are all coming from a place of FEAR.

These behaviours are not examples of confident women taking their position in the world; they are clear examples of desperately insecure people attempting to bring others down or making them feel smaller to give themselves a pathetic little ego boost.   *Whitney*

Now, I'm not sharing these stories to unsettle or upset you. My purpose here is to highlight the negative consequences that happen when courage GOES WRONG.

Journal time

AN INVESTIGATION OF TOXIC FEMININITY IN MY WORLD

I wonder if you've ever encountered someone with toxic femininity. Have you ever worked with, lived with or met a woman who had an exaggerated, twisted, dysfunctional version of courage and confidence?

Karen S.
6th grade

You and I might call her a narcissist, a nightmare or a bitch. Yep, I used the B word.

Cast your mind back over your life history, focusing on the women who have had a negative impact on you. Perhaps, in their presence, you felt:

- insignificant
- embarrassed
- humiliated
- worthless
- amateur
- inexperienced
- underqualified
- fearful
- unsafe.

I hope there are not too many women like this in your memory. For any that do come to mind, I'd like you to reflect on the following:

- What did she typically say?
- What did she typically do?
- How did other people describe her?
- How did you feel in her presence?

Next, after reflecting on this woman's behaviour, in your journal finish these statements:

- When courage goes wrong . . .
- It's so important to demonstrate courage with **empathy**, **tolerance** and **respect** because . . .

So, what then is the opposite of toxic femininity?

We all suspect we need to tap into our courage if we are to fulfil our potential in our careers, relationships and lives. But how can we do this while also showing empathy, compassion and respect?

How can we be authentically courageous women in a world that rewards us for either *knowing our place* or *cutting other women down*?

ENTER: SMART COURAGE

Smart Courage = emotional bravery + intellectual savviness

Emotional bravery is about considering the full emotional impact of a decision, addressing your own emotional needs and the impact on the feelings of others. **Intellectual savviness** is about thinking a decision through in a thorough fashion, weighing up pros and cons, considering implications and looking beyond the immediate situation.

Let's break this down.

Back in the late nineties, I was working in a corporate consulting role. Suited and booted, I'd turn up to work every day in my little pin-striped suit and perfectly groomed hair and nails. I was wearing what felt like a 'corporate costume', playing a role every day in order to get ahead. But I wasn't satisfied – far from it! My passions lay on the stage. Most nights I'd race out of the shiny office, swap my suit for a pair of 'dance pants' (don't judge, it was the nineties!) and head to a dusty, cold, old rehearsal space somewhere in the suburbs. This was my happy place.

One overcast Melbourne morning, while making one of my frequent escapes out of the office on a 'coffee run', I had what I thought was a brilliant epiphany. I'd ask my boss if I could go part-time in my role and spend half of my time pursuing a career in the performing arts. Brilliant, I thought!

I pitched my (what could only be described as 'half-arsed') proposal to him.

The result?

It clearly communicated to my boss that my motivation was sub-par, my focus was elsewhere and I couldn't be trusted to deliver the results he required.

My feelings?

Ashamed, embarrassed, belittled and very, very demotivated.

On reflection now, I can see that this was an example of emotional bravery *without* intellectual savviness. While I had the guts to ask for what I wanted and considered the emotional upside (big tick), I didn't think it through in a sophisticated or even logical manner. I failed to rationalise the proposal or think it through in terms of the impact on the business. It was intellectually dull and ultimately failed.

Fast-forward another three years and I found myself in yet another, still underwhelming, corporate consulting role. It was just after the turn of the century and I felt big things were coming – I knew this was MY TIME. This was my opportunity to break out of the nine-to-five slog and start my own company!

This time, I did think it through (quite thoroughly, I'd say). I planned my move carefully, ensuring I'd have clients and revenue locked in for a few months. I was proud of myself for learning from my previous career-limiting decisions and being more rational and cautious. But this time, I didn't consider the emotional impact.

As a people-person and lover of collaboration, I've always embraced teamwork. For me, there is nothing more satisfying than banding together to share resources and work towards a common goal. To this day, teamwork gives me a real buzz.

The result?

I stepped out of the close-knit team-based environment and into my bedroom/desk space, and quickly realised something was amiss. I hated working alone!

My feelings?

Bored, under-stimulated, flat and very, very demotivated.

So this time, on reflection, I can see that this move demonstrated intellectual savviness *without* emotional bravery. How can you be emotionally brave if you are not self-aware enough to recognise one of your basic social needs?

Over the years, I've come to realise that to step into real courage, it's absolutely critical to draw on your emotional bravery *as well as* your intellectual savviness. Remember:

Smart Courage = emotional bravery + intellectual savviness

Journal time

SMART COURAGE SELF-ANALYSIS

Recall a real situation in your life when you made an important decision (and felt really brave). Now, I'd like you to focus on the things you told yourself at the time (cognitive), the feelings you experienced (emotional) and the things you actually did (behavioural).

Create two columns on the page with the headings:

- Emotional bravery
- Intellectual savviness

Holding the memory of your courageous decision in your mind, write down everything you can remember for each category.

A reminder: **emotional bravery** is about considering the full emotional impact of the decision, addressing your own emotional needs and the impact on the feelings of others. **Intellectual savviness** is about thinking the decision through in a thorough fashion, weighing up pros and cons, considering implications and looking beyond the immediate situation.

What do you notice about the two columns? Are they even? Do you show a clear bias towards the thinking or the feeling elements of the decision?

On balance, would you say that you demonstrated Smart Courage on this occasion? If not, what could you have done differently to demonstrate Smart Courage?

What aspect of your life today could benefit from the application of Smart Courage?

BRAIN DOMINANCE DEBUNKED

When I started formulating the concept of emotional bravery and intellectual savviness, I drew on a theory I'd been using for years: brain dominance theory. This theory states that the brain's two hemispheres function in different ways and was developed by neuropsychologist and Nobel Prize winner Roger W. Sperry in the sixties.

To me, using this theory made sense – some people may be more predisposed to either emotional bravery *or* intellectual savviness in their courageous choices, based on their brain-hemisphere dominance. To my reasoning, if they were more left-brained they would be more inclined to favour an intellectually savvy approach and if they were more right-brained, then they would more likely be emotionally brave.

Sperry's mid-century research found that the left brain hemisphere was linked to logical and practical cognitive functions such as mathematics, dealing with facts and sorting through patterns, while the right brain hemisphere was linked to more visual and intuitive functions like imagination, reading non-verbal cues, interpreting rhythm and daydreaming. In 2013, however, scientists at the University of Utah essentially debunked Sperry's work when they discovered that the human brain doesn't actually favour one side or the other.[9]

So, we could say that 'brain dominance' as a concept does not actually exist – we *all* have capacity for both rational and emotional thought. We may tend to favour one over the other as we develop, based on what feels more natural or is just easier, and this becomes a habit over time. The habit becomes a preference and this influences our approach.

After reading the 2013 Utah research, I changed my opinion. Rather than referring to left-brain and right-brain thinking, I now recognise the importance of nurturing both types of thinking and, especially, focusing on the one that feels less natural.

I don't know about you, but I have to confess to using brain dominance theory as an excuse over the years. I have always believed that I am right-brain dominant (based on behavioural rather than neurological testing) and, therefore, I naturally tend to pay more attention to ideas, feelings and big-picture possibilities. I become easily bored by details, numbers and structures and, as a result, often make mistakes. Sometimes, big ones. It's quite a regular occurrence for me to book a flight for the wrong week, a hotel in the wrong city or turn up to a concert that happened a week ago (not even joking!).

So let's leave our discussion of brain dominance to the side and simply focus on two types of thinking that are both critical for Smart Courage: rational thinking (which I call intellectual savviness) and emotional thinking (AKA emotional bravery).

Reflect back on the Smart Courage self-analysis you completed above.

When you look at your two columns, where did most of your thoughts, feelings and behaviours sit? Mostly intellectual savviness or mostly emotional bravery?

Here are a set of questions to use when you are deciding whether or not to act courageously. Based on your self-analysis, you'll know which side of the ledger needs extra attention, so pay particular attention to the questions that will help you bring greater balance to your approach

Being courageous requires

self-awareness, intelligence, empathy

AND THE WILLINGNESS to see the 40 per cent gap . . . AND JUMP.

naturally focus more on the rational, intellectual savviness
re attention to the emotional bravery side, and vice versa).

Rational processing + intellectual savviness:

- Is the risk worth the reward?
- Does this decision align with my values and broader life goals?
- Do I have all the resources I need to take the first step and sustain this decision?

Emotional processing + emotional bravery:

- Does this feel right? Am I intuitively aligned with this?
- What fears are coming up for me and how will I manage them?
- How will this decision impact my identity and my relationship with my future self?

TIP: Write these questions in your journal for easy reference or bookmark this page and return to it each time you prepare to take courageous action.

HOW DOES IT FEEL TO BE COURAGEOUS?

I'm not going to lie to you – stepping into courage can feel intensely scary.

As humans, we are wired for routine. We like to feel safe in the knowledge that aspects of our lives are predictable. We prefer to understand where we have been, where we are at and where we are going. We like to feel 'in control' of our day-to-day existence and we know that our anxiety levels are generally lower when life is stable.

We have become creatures of habit because it's evolutionarily beneficial to form habits. We tend to connect positive feelings with familiarity, and how is familiarity gained? By doing something over and over again. It's easy to see how a predictable, stable, consistent lifestyle can become a self-perpetuating cycle.

When we form habits, routines and rituals it helps us feel safe and whole. So, it's not at all surprising that taking courageous action (especially when done without the techniques you'll learn in the next chapters) can be daunting. It can feel like you are switching off the lights and jumping off a cliff into the dark unknown.

Making the brave decision to be different, to poke your head above the masses and squint up at the glass ceiling can quite literally lead you towards an extraordinary life.

But it can also scare the sh*t out of you!

Like all situations in life, we can choose to focus on helpful or unhelpful forces when considering the option of being courageous.

Some of the common *unhelpful* cognitive reactions to the prospect of being courageous include:

- talking yourself out of it ('This won't work because . . .')
- giving yourself reasons to 'stay small'
- making excuses to avoid taking action (too busy/not ready/too inexperienced/too fat/too poor)
- telling yourself you don't deserve it ('No one in my family has ever done this, so why should I?')
- inventing reasons why you won't succeed
- procrastinating and creating barriers to action
- convincing yourself you don't really want it
- glorifying the positives of your current, safe situation
- exaggerating the risks of taking action.

And some of the common *unhelpful* emotional reactions to the prospect of being courageous include:

- fear
- embarrassment
- shame
- nervousness
- excitement
- anxiety.

So, ask yourself these questions:

> A – Do you want to be the nice girl who always feels comfortable and in control, lives a mediocre life with satisfactory relationships, has achievable goals and an okay career? A girl who may be remembered for being nice and kind, but not rocking the boat?

Or:

> B – Are you ready to be a woman who pushes her own boundaries, who dares to see herself as something more than mediocre, who strives to excel in her career, achieve her life goals and enjoy abundant, inspiring relationships? A woman who will make a positive, sustainable impact on the world and leave a legacy for the women following in her wake?

I'm going to be totally frank with you here – if you honestly answered A, you can put this book down right now. I'll send you on your way with love and respect, but I'm going to let you know that the remainder of this book is likely to be unsettling and uncomfortable for you. And you may not be ready to read it just yet. And that's okay – you'll become ready in your own time.

If you answered B, read on!

SMART
COURAGE

CHAPTER 5

TIME TO PUT ON YOUR

Big Girl Pants

(WITH AN EXTRA-COMFORTABLE GUSSET)

I had been running my own business for about a year when I started joining forces with a friend and former colleague, Prue. Both psychologists at the time, we had worked together on a range of projects and had (very) different styles – our skill-sets complemented each other beautifully. I loved doing the creative, people-focused work and she enjoyed the more operational, commercial side of things. #yinandyang

One afternoon, while having coffee with one of the fabulous women in my network, I heard that one of the big four banks was unhappy with their current graduate assessment and recruitment provider and they were looking to make a change. At first I let this information wash over me – what did it have to do with me? I was just a single consultant, not even in the same ballpark as the huge, global player currently doing this work.

Later that night I got to thinking. Sure, I couldn't take on a project of this size on my own, but Prue and I had proven time and time again that we were an unbeatable team on large projects. What if we went in on this tender together? What if we joined forces and JUST SAID YES, then figured out the details later?

What if we jumped, then built our parachute on the way down?

I pitched the idea to Prue and she was up for the challenge. So, we created the most impressive proposal we could. We went 'all in' without worrying about the HOW – we decided IF (and it was a huge IF) we won the work, we'd figure out the details then. We knew it was a long shot and, given the bank was accustomed to working with big global players, we genuinely didn't expect it to go any further.

And then it did. We were invited in to pitch our proposal to a panel of six bankers. On our way to the meeting, dressed in our most serious pin-striped suits, we made a pact with each other that we'd project a professional, serious tone (this was not the forum for our typical, casually hilarious style).

Within ten minutes of starting our pitch we had the panel in stitches! So much for our pact. We had naturally slipped into our relaxed communication rhythm, throwing jokes to the panel, bouncing off each other and sharing our expertise in a confident and engaging way. Quite simply, we were just being ourselves. We had nothing to lose.

Three weeks later we got the call – they wanted to work with *us*! They had chosen 'little old Mel and Prue' over a global consulting firm with years of proven results behind them.

We were unknown, untested and unafraid.

So, we mobilised. Within about six weeks we incorporated as a company, hired a project team of 30 consultants around Australia, took on an office lease and invested heavily in the materials we'd need to deliver the project. As we were an unknown commercial entity, we couldn't get access to finance, so we had to raise the cash ourselves. And we did it!

This project turned into a three-year engagement and our business became a huge success. Who would've thought? We would.

This experience would become a defining moment in my life. It was the first time I really seriously backed myself and took the risk to expand my comfort zone. One thing I've learned is that most women, even high-achieving women, respond better to opportunities to *expand* their comfort zone, rather than *leave* it altogether.

When I look back at the bank project with Prue, I think the reason we were successful was not because we jumped without a parachute, but because we'd built a safety harness to guide us to the parachute and beyond.

We did not leave our comfort zone, we expanded it.

EXPAND YOUR COMFORT ZONE

I've discovered that five factors need to be in place for you to expand your comfort zone in a safe, enjoyable and low-anxiety way:

1. **Emotional bravery** – Prue and I talked at length about our emotional needs in pitching for this project. We discussed how it would impact our personal lives, our mental health and our relationship as business partners. We mapped out stress-management strategies and ensured we'd have outlets when things got tough (daily walks around a nearby lake played a big role in this).

2. **Intellectual savviness** – We spent many hours thinking through the logistics and practical aspects of the project. We had spreadsheets, graphs and apps to support the project and even engaged a business coach to guide us through the commercial aspects of our business growth.

3. **Self-esteem** – We had no doubt that we deserved this project (once we got over the initial shock!). We believed we were worthy and were more than prepared to be put to the test.

4. **Self-efficacy** – We had a good track record to draw on. We'd done this kind of work before (although not on this large scale) and we trusted our ability as a team. We never doubted our capability.

5. **Social support** – Not only did we have each other, we surrounded ourselves with a highly capable team who all shared our vision. We felt supported each step of the way, which made the tough times less scary. Outside the business, we had family and friends who cheered us on from the sidelines.

Of course, we had stressful moments and at times it felt too big to manage. But our new, expanded comfort zone was there to soften the impact and keep us on the right track.

THE COMFORT OF COMFORT

What happens when someone tells you to *step outside your comfort zone*?

- Your anxiety goes up.
- Fear creeps in.
- Self-doubts start to build.
- Resistance abounds.

I've certainly been guilty of spouting this command to clients and friends in the past. But not anymore – I've realised that this is not only unhelpful but, more often than not, ineffective.

When someone tells you to step outside your comfort zone, they are essentially saying:

> Turn your back on all the support systems and confidence-boosting mechanisms you have spent your whole life building up. Walk away from your safety net and risk everything to try something new.

Instantly, your mindset shifts from 'I am capable and I deserve success' (coming from a place of security and a level of certainty) to 'I am uncertain and not sure if the next step is right for me' (coming from a place of ambiguity and less clarity).

But does this have to be the case?

ANXIETY AND COURAGE ARE COUSINS

They are intimately connected, but not by choice. Without fear and anxiety, there can be no courage.

I'm sorry to say that, without a level of psychological tension, a courageous act is not a courageous act. It's just an act.

While we may allow ourselves to view anxiety as a 'necessary evil' when it comes to moving into courage, we don't have to like it. And to make it worse, we women have been shown to experience more anxiety than men.

Research has found that, by the age of six, girls are twice as likely as boys to have experienced an anxiety disorder.[10]

Think about what this means for us – during our critical, formative years from babyhood to six, twice as many of us have to grapple with anxiety than our male playmates. Imagine the impact on not only our developing brains, but also our social development and capacity to believe in ourselves and trust our instincts.

Now, this book is not a clinical text, so we won't be delving into anxiety disorders here. But I do think it's important that we think about anxiety in the 'normal range' as it applies in our everyday life. I'm talking about those annoying, common, garden-variety worries that most of us experience, as opposed to serious anxiety that requires treatment.

According to the brilliant Australian mental health resource hub Beyond Blue, anxiety is the most common mental health condition in the country. At some point in their life, one in four people – one in three women and one in five men – will experience anxiety. And each year, more than two million Australians experience anxiety.[11]

So, how do you tell if your anxiety is *not* in the normal range? Normal anxiety tends to be limited in time and connected with a particular stressful situation or event, such as a job interview, first date, family argument or the wait for medical results. With normal anxiety, you can usually pinpoint exactly what has triggered you and put strategies in place to manage it. However, if your anxiety doesn't go away once an event is over, if it happens for no obvious reason or if it's making your life really challenging, then it may be the sign of an anxiety condition.[12]

Different anxiety conditions have their own specific features, but, according to Beyond Blue, there are some common symptoms to look out for:

- **Physical** – panic attacks, hot and cold flushes, racing heart, tightening of the chest, quick breathing, restlessness, or feeling tense, wound up and edgy

- **Psychological** – excessive fear, worry, catastrophising or obsessive thinking
- **Behavioural** – avoidance of situations that make you feel anxious, which can impact on study, work or social life.[13]

If you experience any of these symptoms for longer than two weeks and you believe they stop you from getting on with your life, consult your GP and ask for a referral to a psychologist. Beyond Blue is also a great resource: beyondblue.org.au/the-facts/anxiety.

FROM ANXIETY TO ACTION

I think we all agree that a level of anxiety is a part of modern life. The real question here is what can we do about it.

How do we stop anxiety from getting in the way of our courageous pursuits? How do we nip anxious thoughts in the bud to enable ourselves to move through them and into a state of strength and preparedness for action?

One of the most common self-sabotaging trains of thought is known as Catastrophic Thinking. This is turning a minor situation into a full-blown, worst-case scenario through your thoughts and fantasies. This type of negative thought spiral can take you from 'I can't do this' to 'If I do this, my world will implode'.

Catastrophic thinking and the accompanying anxiety can undermine your ability to think or act courageously, so you need to put it in its place.

Remember my old mate, Cognitive Behavioural Therapy (CBT)? CBT techniques really come in handy when getting ready to take courageous action.

Let's say you are about to give an important presentation to a boardroom of judgmental colleagues . . .

Your internal monologue goes something like this:

> I'm not ready for this, I haven't prepared enough. When I
> stand up I'll probably start shaking or stuttering. Everyone will
> see that I'm going red and sweating and they'll think I'm an
> amateur. They'll wonder what I'm doing giving a presentation
> and call me out for all my mistakes. My boss will see that I
> don't deserve to be in this position and she will sack me.
> I won't be able to afford my rent and I'll become homeless.
> Who will love me when I'm homeless?

Okay, this may be a little extreme but you get the picture. This catastrophic style of thinking may lead to emotional states such as:

- fear
- angst
- embarrassment
- shame
- dread
- feeling out of control
- feeling like you can't cope
- a strong urge to run away.

If you imagine yourself playing out this monologue and experiencing these emotions, I'm sure you can predict the likely behavioural outcomes. Probably not a rousing round of applause and a promotion, right?

So, what can you do if or when catastrophic thinking starts to emerge?

1. **Stop and breathe** – If you can't physically remove yourself from the situation, try taking a couple of deep, slow, intentional breaths. Mentally remove yourself from the room for a moment, visualise you are somewhere else if you need to. Give yourself a little space. It also helps to say out loud (or write it if you're in company) the word STOP!

2. **Take a beat** – Give yourself a moment to assess the situation and your thinking patterns (remember we talked about metacognition – observing and assessing your thoughts will make a powerful difference). Evaluate your thinking and try to cool yourself down. Saying something to yourself like 'It's just anxiety' or 'These are anxious thoughts and I can replace them with something more helpful' will help.

3. **Challenge your thoughts** – Look for evidence that the catastrophic thoughts are real. Are people 'actually' laughing at you? Are you 'really' underprepared? Be firm and honest with yourself.

4. **Reframe your thoughts** – Choose a different, more constructive and self-enhancing way to look at the situation. Change your internal narrative to something like 'This is a new situation so it's natural to feel nervous, but I've done a similar presentation before and I know I can do this. I'm well-prepared and I know my team is on board with these ideas. I simply have to show them.'

5. **Start again** – Hold your reframed thoughts in your mind as you re-enter the situation. Allow the normal 'nerves' of the presentation to happen then move past them to deliver the goods.

BIG GIRL PANTS VS BIG BOY PANTS

We are constantly bombarded by strong messages about destroying our comfort zone in order to get ahead. Part of living within a patriarchal society means many of the unconscious cultural cues we receive every day are masculine in tone, energy and focus.

Commercial slogans like Nike's 'Just do it' and aspects of our everyday vernacular such as 'Go big or go home' communicate the urgency of breaking down our resistance to change.

While these messages may be motivating for some women, the vast majority of us tend to shut down or avoid head-on challenges to our safety and sense of security in life.

Let's not pretend men and women are built the same.

When it comes to brain chemistry and the hormones that determine our motivation levels, we are poles apart. Men tend to have more testosterone (the competition and assertiveness hormone) surging through their veins and this leads to a greater tendency towards:

- power roles
- status seeking
- risk-taking
- competitiveness
- dominance and aggression
- visual-spatial tasks.

Women tend to have more oxytocin (the bonding hormone) underpinning our behaviour, which often leads to a greater tendency towards:

- prosocial acts
- trust-building
- emotional connection
- emotional adaptation
- communication.

No wonder women are more attuned to slogans like L'Oréal's 'Because you're worth it'. Typically, women respond well to messages that lift our esteem, build us up and enable connection with others.

I don't know about you, but this is so evident for me when it comes to fitness training. I was once a part of a bootcamp group training program with a commando-style leader. He would shout, literally shout at us to move our bodies. He would use threats and light humiliation, and pit us against each other. If one person lagged behind, he would single them out and make the whole group suffer for their weakness, thus further compounding the humiliation and individualised goals. Talking and slacking off were forbidden.

After four weeks in this program, I would rate my fitness results as 3 out of 10.

Another time, a close girlfriend and I worked as a pair with a trainer who had a very different style. She would encourage and praise us whenever she could. She would celebrate our wins and enable us to play to our strengths. We would laugh and chat and build our relationships as we trained. We discussed and agreed on both individual and shared goals, building the sense that we were in this together.

After four weeks in this program, I'd rate my fitness results as 9 out of 10.

And I don't think I'm alone on this.

THE COMFORT ZONE VS THE ANXIETY ZONE

You might have come across wellness or motivational influencers saying things like 'Everything you want is on the other side of fear' or 'Nothing good ever happened within your comfort zone'. While I get the sentiment, on the whole I don't believe these messages are motivating or helpful for women.

As we've discussed, the idea of removing ourselves from a comfortable and safe space often initiates a fear response. This is our natural self-preservation kicking in.

So, if I'm told to abandon the things that make me feel secure in order to step into the unfamiliar, it's likely to provoke anxiety. As we know by now, if I'm feeling stressed or under pressure I'll likely go into fight, flight or freeze mode, become flooded with unhelpful chemicals and lose the capacity to think clearly.

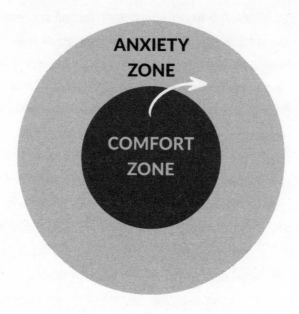

Try something with me:

> Imagine your comfort zone as a luxurious room, the Comfort Room. Soft fluffy couches and cushions envelop you, your favourite colour scheme surrounds you, it's the perfect temperature, your favourite music plays, all your favourite people are there and, most importantly, you feel in control, calm and confident.
>
> Now, imagine someone comes along and tells you that in order to get what you want in life, you must step out of this room and into the Anxiety Room. In here, you'll find uncomfortable stools that are too high and harsh, bright lights. Loud music will be blaring and you'll be confronted by people and experiences who push your buttons (and not in a good way).

Does the Anxiety Room sound like a smart way to improve your confidence, happiness and success in life? Probably not. Acting from a place of safety and comfort – your Comfort Room – helps you step into courage.

Rather than a full-blown fear response and high anxiety (both of which would be waiting for you in the Anxiety Room), you'll most likely feel manageable anxiety or moderate fear (or perhaps even excitement!).

This feeling can be used to your advantage, because one of the things sports psychology and professional athletes have taught us is that a moderate level of arousal promotes the best performance.

That is, fear and anxiety only motivate us to a certain point, then, beyond that, our performance drops. It's called the Yerkes–Dodson Law, after the two psychologists who hypothesised it. So to be our best, to maximise our performance potential, we need to operate with a moderate level of arousal – not boredom and not panic but the optimal point between the two.

'I'M BORED'	'I'M READY FOR ACTION'		'I'M PANICKING'	
1	2	3	4	5	6	7	8	9	10

Now you might call this arousal anxiety, fear or stress, but I prefer to give it a neutral name: energy. It's neither positive nor negative, it's simply energy. It manifests in the form of physical, mental and emotional arousal.

Just like when midwives refer to contractions as 'surges', we can take the sting out of the terminology. Words have so much power over our emotional responses so when we choose to use neutral language for otherwise threatening situations, we lessen their power. We discussed this when talking about fear – rather than saying 'I'm scared', say 'I'm excited'. It may seem like semantics but it can change your entire psychological and physiological response.

So, how can you continue to have a base level of safety, while also taking risks that raise your energy to manageable levels?

SPOTLIGHT ON PIPPA |
EXPAND YOUR COMFORT ZONE

I'd like to introduce you to a woman I'll call Pippa. When we met, Pippa had spent 15 years as a banker – a straight-talking, tough-minded, highly analytical numbers woman. She had dedicated herself to her career, progressed up the corporate ladder because 'that's what you do' and had carved out a very successful and lucrative career.

But she was miserable.

By throwing herself into her career, Pippa had missed out on aspects of life – holidays with the girls, long weekends away, days at the races and flirty dates. She had essentially put her social life on hold to allow her career to flourish.

And then there was her health.

By putting her work first, Pippa had neglected her health and fitness and had spiralled into an unhealthy, sedentary lifestyle of takeaway food, alcohol, late nights and couch dwelling.

The turning point

By the time she reached 36, Pippa was burnt-out. Unhealthy. Unfit. Unhappy. And alone

Something had to give.

At around the same time, Pippa's cousin was diagnosed with a chronic illness that was largely lifestyle related. This was the wake-up call Pippa needed to re-evaluate her life and take stock of her past, present and future.

We worked together on Pippa's life evaluation and I guided her through a few activities that helped her tap into her deepest desires, strengths, passions and values.

Pippa soon discovered that the life she had been living was completely out of alignment with who she really was and what she really wanted.

When we stripped away her 'corporate persona', Pippa realised she was a person who really valued health, who wanted to live a vital life and who had a strong desire to help people.

The butterfly emerges

With Pippa's values, strengths and life goals in mind, we worked together to develop a plan to expand her comfort zone. Pippa knew that doing something drastic (like quitting her job and joining an ashram in India) might feel good in the moment but wouldn't lead to her long-term happiness. So we explored ways to gently push the boundaries of her comfort zone to enable it to expand. Pippa's courageous (yet rather comfortable) actions included:

- finishing work at a reasonable time twice a week so she could prioritise a yoga class
- walking to and from work two days per week, with one of these days involving a 'walk and talk' with a workmate
- engaging a nutrition specialist to help her make small and sustainable changes to her diet – this new knowledge gave Pippa the confidence to start meal prepping and taking her own healthy lunch to work
- starting to say NO more in the professional environment, setting new and clear boundaries about her workload.

Pippa chose to expand her zone of comfort by bringing new things into the place she already felt comfortable. Nothing dramatic or extreme, these were all things she felt at ease with.

Fast-forward six months and Pippa fundamentally changed her life.

She started studying yoga teaching, transitioned out of her job, overhauled her diet and lost 17 kilos.

She was well on track to becoming a yoga teacher with big dreams about opening her own studio, a nurturing space for women to relax and flourish.

Pippa also joined her local gym during this transitional time in her life and started to connect with a different group of people. Rather than restricting her interactions to work colleagues, she was now mixing with fit, motivated and energetic people who really resonated with her true self.

By Christmas that year, about nine months into her journey, Pippa was feeling completely different about her career, her health, her future and herself. She was looking at her life through a new lens, a much more optimistic lens that stimulated excitement, anticipation and motivation.

She agreed to attend the gym Christmas party (something the old Pippa would have avoided) and bought a new dress for the occasion.

As she approached the venue she noticed that she felt different – calm, poised, proud, confident and, most of all, excited about what the night may bring.

This was a very new feeling for her and she loved it.

During her evening, Pippa found herself chatting with Chin, one of the guys from her pump class. She had noticed his friendly smile a few times before, but had never had the courage to say hello.

As the night wore on, she realised they were only speaking to each other and it was like everyone else had disappeared!

This was the first time she had ever been so comfortable speaking with a man in a social setting. It came so easily for her as they had so much in common – they both valued health, fitness and family, both enjoyed an active lifestyle and both wanted to help others and make the planet a better place.

Needless to say, they had a lot to talk about.

At the end of the night, Chin asked Pippa out and she happily accepted the date. Her first *real* date.

Today

Pippa is working as a yoga teacher, living an active, healthy life, with Chin by her side.

Now approaching 40, she has started investigating fertility options and she and Chin are planning a family.

Pippa says that Chin is her ideal, perfect partner. He knows when to support her and when to allow her to be independent, he gives her space when she needs it and smothers her with love when she needs that too. They have fun together, they play, they run, they hike and they cook healthy food together.

What can we learn from Pippa's story?

Pippa created a 'happily ever after' in her life by identifying the need to *expand her comfort zone*.

She evaluated her life, recognised where changes needed to happen, invested in making those changes and had the courage to back herself in her life change.

And boy, did it pay off!

•

By defining your goals and taking gentle steps towards them, you will set the scene for an authentic life. When you are living your values and being true to yourself, you will start to connect with people who share similar values and lifestyle preferences.

Like attracts like.

So take a leaf out of Pippa's book and start investing in yourself. Ask yourself what you could change about your life to be more aligned with your core values or your greatest passions, and consider what you could do to expand your zone of comfort.

EXPAND YOUR ROOM – THE COURAGEOUS MINDSET

What if I told you that you can improve your confidence, happiness and success in life while staying safely in your Comfort Room?

Of course, a few things will need to change, but *you* are in control of exactly what changes. The beauty of your own, custom-built Comfort Room is that it's completely flexible and adaptable.

Imagine your Comfort Room expanding in response to your need for growth.

Rather than stepping outside it, you choose to bring new things *into* the room. Now, you find that your new experiences are held within your warm, secure and comfortable place, rather than you having to go out into the cold, stark Anxiety Room in order to try them.

Imagine bringing the things that stretch you and encourage your growth into your Comfort Room. You might see your room expanding as you add a treadmill, a new workplace, a different relationship or a different-shaped body.

Here's how it can work in practice.

EXAMPLE 1: YOU DECIDE YOU WANT TO LEAVE YOUR NINE-TO-FIVE JOB AND START YOUR OWN FLORIST SHOP.

JUMPING INTO THE ANXIETY ROOM	EXPANDING YOUR COMFORT ROOM
• Resign from your job, effective immediately. • You celebrate! • Look for a vacant shop to lease. • Research flower suppliers. • Consider some business systems. Three months later . . . • You haven't found an appropriate shop to rent. • You realise the floral industry is more complicated than you thought. • You're running out of savings. • You're wondering how you're going to pay your mortgage. • Stress and anxiety are rapidly rising. • You have no idea what to do next.	• You decide to go part-time in your nine-to-five job, giving you two days each week to research your business. • You line up a shop, connect with industry bodies, start networking and learning the ropes. • You research and test all your business systems. Three months later . . . • Resign from your job, giving one month's notice to gather some extra savings. • After one month, you move into your new business with most of the ground work already done. • You feel calm, excited and a little nervous. • You celebrate!

EXAMPLE 2: YOU FEEL YOU NEED TO 'BREAK UP' WITH A LONG-TIME FRIEND.

JUMPING INTO THE ANXIETY ROOM	EXPANDING YOUR COMFORT ROOM
• You confront her while out for drinks. • Given you've had a few, you share more than you planned to about all the things she does to annoy you. • You become flustered and have trouble getting your point across. • You really hurt her feelings and leave her feeling confused and completely rejected. • She gets angry and leaves the bar. • You never see her again. Three months later . . . • You miss her terribly. • You constantly wonder what she's up to. • You feel too embarrassed and ashamed to reach out to her. • Your anxiety skyrockets.	• You start journaling about the friendship, helping you gain clarity about what is working and not working for you. • You become crystal-clear about the pros and cons, ultimately realising that the friendship does not serve you. • You move her from the A list to the B list in your friendship sphere – this means you start setting clearer boundaries with her and start to limit the amount of emotional vulnerability you share. Three months later . . . • You have gradually taken a step back from the friendship. • You only see her occasionally and keep her at arm's length emotionally. • You feel relieved and empowered.

EXAMPLE 3: YOU DECIDE TO MOVE OVERSEAS.

JUMPING INTO THE ANXIETY ROOM	EXPANDING YOUR COMFORT ROOM
• You buy an open plane ticket. • You tell your loved ones your plans. • You fly to your first destination and start your adventure. Three months later . . . • You haven't found anywhere that really lights you up. • You haven't been able to connect with like-minded travellers yet. • It's hard to get around, not knowing the language. • You feel a little lost and anxious about what you're doing with your life.	• You do your research and decide to relocate to Italy. • You spend time learning the language and familiarising yourself with the culture. • You join online groups and connect with other travellers who have a passion for Italy. • You start networking with Italian connections in your career stream. Three months later . . . • You land in Rome and travel to your rented apartment on the Amalfi Coast. • You spend the first month socialising, eating, learning to cook Italian food and getting to know your community. • You start a new job. • You feel grounded, strong and excited about the future.

As I'm sure you noticed, these are great examples of Smart Courage. Each one balances intellectual savviness (research, testing out new things, building relevant skills, connecting with relevant networks) and emotional bravery (building new relationships for support and connection, protecting yourself from emotional vulnerabilities, setting clear boundaries).

Now, I'm not saying there is no room for spontaneity. This is not about taking the fun out of life or getting old before your time. Quite the contrary. Expanding your comfort zone is about giving yourself the gift of space and time to move at your own pace, have some successes along the way and build confidence as you go – rather than jumping in head first and possibly drowning!

THE EXPANDED COMFORT ZONE TAKES GUTS

In the first instance, you might be thinking, 'This expanded comfort zone business is too soft for me, I want to do big things in life and I'm in a hurry.' To this, I would say 'Slow down and take a closer look . . . this is the best way to toughen up and take risks.'

When compared with jumping into the anxiety zone, expanding your comfort zone will give you more opportunity to build resilience. In many ways, jumping into the anxiety zone is the easy way, the quick fix that might provide some instant gratification but will ultimately do little to progress your life. Stepping into the anxiety zone rarely gives you the opportunity to grow, expand and build your psychological skills. Remember, when you're in a state of heightened anxiety, you have limited capacity for thinking clearly, connecting with others, making decisions, having perspective or reflecting on your own behaviour.

By expanding your comfort zone, you'll have the time, space and energy to make mistakes, fall down, get back up and try again. Only through this iterative process will you build resilience – the ultimate in psychological flexibility.

Resilience refers to the capacity to bounce back after a fall.

When you constantly place yourself in situations that induce anxiety, you are essentially robbing yourself of the opportunity to learn and build resilience. In psychological terms, resilience is the superpower of the mentally strong.

Expanding your comfort zone is not the soft option. It's the *smart* option.

Journal time

COMFORT ROOM VISUALISATION

Take a moment to relax and calmly picture your Comfort Room in your mind.

1. Imagine your Comfort Room – fill in all the details and make sure you cover all of your five senses. Allow yourself to really experience all the emotions that come up for you here; indulge in the security, warmth and comforting hug this room provides.
2. Think about an area of your life that you would like to develop – be extremely specific with your goal.
3. Imagine bringing things that represent this goal into your Comfort Room. Really see them physically placed in your room.
4. Notice how it feels to see these things in your safe, comfortable place. Take note of how you need to adapt your mindset, your feelings and your response to your goal.
5. Now, sit in your Comfort Room, with your new things, and contemplate your first steps towards change. Notice that you feel in control, calm and quietly excited about the new experience you are about to create.

Take some time to reflect on this visualisation in your journal. What other goals could you apply this technique to? This slight change in approach can help you to feel (and be) more in control when it comes to your personal growth. The Comfort Room technique will give you more agency and a greater internal sense of control when deciding to expand your world.

EXPANDING YOUR

comfort zone

is not the

SOFT OPTION.

It's the

SMART OPTION.

THE COSTS OF STAYING IN YOUR COMFORT ZONE

Here are some questions you may not have considered before:

How expensive is your comfort zone?

What does it COST you to stay there?

WHY are you still there?

Psychologists talk about a thing called *secondary gain* when it comes to the avoidance of personal change. Secondary gain can be described as the benefits people get from *not* overcoming a problem. People aren't usually consciously aware of it; it tends to emerge over time and becomes a crutch.

Sometimes, people become so accustomed to the 'pay-offs' of not changing that they can end up stuck, unable to move forward. Of course, this type of behaviour leads to all sorts of missed opportunities in careers, relationships and life.

I'll illustrate with some examples here, but please note that these are intended to describe the process, not to judge the person (we all have examples of secondary gain in our lives):

- **Staying in an abusive relationship**. Secondary gain = receiving positive attention and sympathy from others due to your role as 'victim'.
- **Not losing weight** (even though your health is at risk). Secondary gain = getting to indulge in your favourite foods every day and not having to exercise because it's too taxing on your body.
- **Remaining in financial debt**. Secondary gain = feeling 'free' to keep spending without taking responsibility for the consequences.

While secondary gains are excuses for staying stuck in an unhealthy rut, they can also disguise the costs of being there. Let's consider the above examples again, this time looking at the associated costs:

- **Staying in an abusive relationship**. Costs = diminished self-esteem, emotional trauma, physical injuries, learned helplessness and missed opportunities for a better relationship and life.
- **Not losing weight** (even though your health is at risk). Costs = increased risk of heart disease, high chance of diabetes, reduced mobility, missed opportunities for physical activities and social events.
- **Remaining in financial debt**. Costs = long-term damage to credit rating, missed opportunities to build wealth and enjoy financial freedom.

Journal time

SECONDARY GAINS AND HIDDEN COSTS

It's time to put yourself under the microscope. I'd like you to think about a time when you opted to stay within your comfort zone for a prolonged period of time. In your journal, respond to these questions:

- What happened?
- What did you do?
- What did you tell yourself about why you were staying there?
- How did it feel to stay there?
- On a scale of 1 to 10, how consciously aware were you that you were stuck?
- What were the secondary gains for you?
- What did it cost you to stay there?
- On reflection, how might you approach a similar situation differently next time?

I hope now you understand what I mean when I say it's time to put on your Big Girl Pants with an extra-comfy gusset. Yes, becoming confident means you need to step into courage with bravery and gumption, but it is possible to do it in a way that nurtures you through the process. Choose to expand your comfort zone rather than step out of it and you'll discover you are more willing – and more capable – to take risks and grow both personally and professionally.

SMART
COURAGE

CHAPTER 6

FROM NICE GIRL TO Courageous Woman

Have you heard of Lois P. Frankel? Even if you're not familiar with her name, you may have come across her groundbreaking book *Nice Girls Don't Get The Corner Office: 101 Unconscious Mistakes Women Make That Sabotage Their Careers*. She wrote the first incarnation of this book in 2004 and, while she has her detractors, she is seen as one of the trailblazers of female empowerment in the career and business space.

> **You gain courage and confidence from doing the things you think you cannot do.**
>
> **LOIS P. FRANKEL**

Frankel identified the socialisation processes that influence us as young girls and the way these lessons go on to become our unconscious (and unhelpful) habits as adult women. According to Frankel, our self-sabotage behaviours start in girlhood. While behaving as an obedient little girl may serve us as kids, similar behaviour in adulthood can be undermining at best, unsafe at worst. She repeatedly urges women to be more assertive in the workplace.

Before we dig any deeper into Frankel's advice, I need to add my ten cents. Her work has been criticised for essentially blaming the woman rather than acknowledging that the system is inherently biased and built to favour men. This is true, and I believe we need to consider her advice within the social context of the time.

For me, it's more about focusing on the things we *can change* (that is, ourselves) while acknowledging that we are operating within a system that we *cannot immediately change* (that is, the sociopolitical environment). This is not about blaming women or men, but honing in on the positive change we can make for our own lives and those of the women who follow us.

Agreed?

To help you build self-awareness, it's worthwhile to examine a sample of the unconscious mistakes Frankel has identified (she lists over a hundred in her book). Consider if any of these feel true for you:

- Mistake #13: Avoiding office politics
- Mistake #21: Multi-tasking
- Mistake #54: Failure to negotiate
- Mistake #82: Asking permission
- Mistake #100: Smiling inappropriately.

At face value, calling these behaviours 'mistakes' seems quite harsh and judgmental, don't you think? But my take on Frankel's work is that she is essentially saying this:

1. Take ownership of your career and the way you show up in the world.

2. Don't behave like a little girl, a slave or a victim.

3. Be self-aware enough to make conscious choices about the way you think, feel, speak and behave.

4. Strategically design your personal brand and make active choices to behave in accordance with your values and goals.

5. Speak up when you are treated unfairly.

6. Value your own time and expertise as much as you value that of others.

For me, these six lessons are the key takeaways from Frankel's work. These fundamental beliefs and attitudes will form a strong foundation for you as you start to design your approach to being a smart, courageous woman.

Once you're clear on your WHY (your mindset), you can consider your HOW – that is, how you start to express your Smart Courage in your career, relationships and life.

BEING A SMART WOMAN

Frankel put forward seven pillars of being a 'Smart Woman' as opposed to being a 'Nice Girl'. Her seven pillars cover how you:

- play the game
- act
- think
- brand and market yourself
- sound
- look
- respond.

Let's take her seven pillars and translate them into the C Word Method approach.

HOW YOU PLAY THE GAME

This is about stepping into the political environment of your workplace or social sphere in a conscious and intentional way. Rather than simply 'going with the flow', it's about setting your intention, making a decision about what you want and what you need to do to achieve your desired outcomes. Without such strategy, you are more inclined to be influenced by others and led away from your true path. When you understand your own values, you'll be in a stronger position to make a call on what is right for YOU in a situation, rather than going with the majority or following the popular vote.

Have you ever agreed to do something then later had regrets?

Ever reflected on a situation and thought 'Why did I agree to do something that wasn't in my own interests?'

Playing the game with strategic intent means you're less likely to have regrets because you are fully present for every decision (more on how to say NO later).

HOW YOU ACT

Ultimately, you will be judged by what you do – that is, how you conduct yourself. Your manner, your energy, your words and behaviours. This is the outward projection of your SELF and, fairly or not, it forms the data that many people will use to form impressions about you.

Have you ever noticed how often western women apologise? There is a tendency for many women to unconsciously apologise for their existence and seek permission in everyday conversation. For example:

- 'Sorry, can I just ask . . .'
- 'Sorry, I'm Jenny. Just wondering if maybe . . .'
- 'Perhaps we could maybe consider . . . No problem if we don't but . . .'

When you are interrupted, try responding with a clear statement like, 'I'm still talking, happy to take questions when I've finished my point.' Many women use filler words such as 'um' or 'so' and these can dilute your messages. You might sometimes add in a 'sooo . . .' to buy yourself some time and nervously fill in a pause; you'd be better off, however, taking an intentional pause and a deep breath while maintaining eye contact with your audience, then picking up where you left off. When you use tentative or hesitant language, you communicate to others that you are unsure of yourself or you don't believe that you deserve the floor.

HOW YOU THINK

For me, this is the most important aspect of Frankel's advice. In fact, everything else on her list comes back to the way you think. As we now know from Cognitive Behavioural Therapy, your thoughts influence the feelings you have, which in turn influence the actions you take.

Your cognitive inner world is the key to mastering your career, relationships and life.

The stories you tell yourself about your competence, worthiness and potential will have a huge impact on the way you show up. The way you talk to yourself about your role and impact in the world will significantly colour the experience you have.

This is where reframing techniques become invaluable. Take a look at these examples of how to reframe what you tell yourself.

AT WORK:

RATHER THAN	TELL YOURSELF
I don't think they'll listen to my ideas.	I've put a lot of thought into these ideas, the team is just as likely to consider my ideas as anyone else's.
I won't put myself forward in case they don't choose me.	I'm putting my hand up – worst-case scenario is they say no and I look for the next opportunity. Best-case scenario is they choose me and I take my career on a new path.

IN RELATIONSHIPS:

RATHER THAN	TELL YOURSELF
I'm not going to bring up the fact that my friend hurt my feelings, it's too uncomfortable.	I'll express how her actions hurt me and gently explain how I'd rather be treated.
I doubt my partner will stick around for long, most of my partners leave me.	This is a good relationship and my partner has strong feelings for me. Despite my track record, I've learned lessons and trust myself to choose the right partners.

Your cognitive

inner world

is the key
to mastering

your career,

relationships

AND LIFE.

U BRAND AND MARKET YOURSELF

igital communication and social media are such critical elements of our lives, the outward expression of our personal and professional brand is more important than ever.

Whether we like it or not, we are communicating our brand 24/7.

Once we have a clear vision of who we are, how we see ourselves within our role, company, industry or social networks, it's easier to present a consistent message. To refine your personal brand, ask yourself:

- What are my three highest values?
- How would I like my peers to describe me?
- How do I want people to feel after they spend time with me?
- What will I leave as a legacy?
- What am I an 'expert' in?

I love Jim Collins' description of the Hedgehog Concept (outlined in his iconic book *Good To Great*) when thinking about personal branding. It's based on a fragment from an ancient Greek parable: 'The fox knows many things, but the hedgehog knows one big thing.' The hedgehog is highly attuned to danger and, when faced with a threat, curls into a tight, impenetrable ball and rolls out of harm's way. The hedgehog's survival technique works every time; it is its defining characteristic – the hedgehog is known for it.

Collins asserts that we need to figure out what we are passionate about, what we can make money from and what we can be the best in the world at. He found that companies (or indeed people) who found their 'one big thing' and focused intently on that were more likely to progress from *good to great*.

So, what can you be the best at? #belikethehedgehog

HOW YOU SOUND

One of Frankel's seven pillars pays particular attention to how we sound, something that can affect how seriously – or not – women are taken in the workplace. Countless research projects have found that women are regularly talked over, interrupted, misunderstood or misheard when they speak, for reasons such as pitch, word selection and social and cultural biases.[14] Women usually speak at a higher pitch than men – about an octave higher.

Have you heard the term 'upspeak' (AKA uptalk, rising inflection or high rising intonation)? It describes the vocal pattern of saying the last syllable of a sentence in a higher voice or intonation, most commonly employed by women. It often results in a statement sounding more like a question. Upspeak can communicate a lack of confidence on behalf of the speaker, and creates the impression that they are less intelligent or sophisticated than they actually are.

Next time you have an important point to make, prepare yourself by intentionally lowering the pitch of your voice, slow down the speed of your speech and become more aware of how you end sentences. Use pauses to underline your point – if someone hijacks your pause, calmly state that you are still talking, and continue.

HOW YOU LOOK

This is a contentious one. In an ideal world, there would be no connection between what women *wear*, how we are *perceived* and what we are said to *deserve*. Unfortunately, we are all too aware of the social connection between our clothing choices and the accusations of 'she was asking for it'. Members of the legal system have been known to interrogate sexual assault survivors on their personal presentation in an attempt to discredit them in court. This is unfair, irrelevant and unreasonable and should be illegal. But here we are.

I experienced an illuminating example of these attitudes when living in Dubai in the late 2000s. In a culture where local women are completely covered, western women were expected to wear a more modest version of our usual business attire. Given the heat (40 to 50 degrees Celsius), I started by wearing a calf-length skirt with a short-sleeved business shirt, with a couple of top buttons undone. Oh, and I wasn't married at the time, so my ring finger was bare. I found that my credibility in the business setting while dressed this way was limited. Men would leer at my uncovered arms and strain their necks to get a glimpse of my calves, and it was impossible to have an eye-to-eye conversation (know what I mean?). Dressed in this fashion, which was a modified version of my Australian business attire, I found that men would openly speak over me, ignore me, blatantly belittle me and overrule any ideas I'd put forward. I gradually adapted my wardrobe to include suit pants and long-sleeved business shirts with all buttons done up (and even borrowed a wedding ring for some meetings) – hardly comfortable in such sweltering heat. Not surprisingly, my mini-experiment of changing my clothes proved my hypothesis correct: men took me more seriously as a business associate when I covered myself up.

Now, you may be living in the western world and possibly wondering why a Middle Eastern example is relevant here. Well, sometimes it helps to give an extreme example to highlight a common problem: the way we look influences people's impressions of us.

While you may not be about to take the witness stand or enter a boardroom in the Gulf, *think* about the messages you are sending via your personal presentation. Be aware of your appearance in different situations, and consider the impact on others. Note, I'm not suggesting you tone down your sexuality or necessarily dress differently, I'm just suggesting you be aware.

Forewarned is forearmed.

I personally believe that intelligence, sexiness, femininity, sophistica-tion, warmth, professionalism and assertiveness can coexist in one woman. And you can choose to express these and other attributes however you please, but smart women like you and me are wise about what we choose to wear, when and why.

HOW YOU RESPOND

Have you ever noticed that many people use the terms 'respond' and 'react' interchangeably?

While on the surface they seem similar, they describe two very different intentions. A **reaction** is considered to be an unconscious, almost knee-jerk retort to a stimulus based on deeply held beliefs, biases and prejudices. A reaction feels like it happens without thinking, it's in the moment and generally doesn't take into account the likely consequences.[15]

A **response** is more intentional. When we respond, we typically take the time to draw on both conscious and unconscious information and take into account short-term and longer-term implications.[16]

If a *reaction* is an impulsive teenager, then a *response* is her more mature, somewhat bookish older sister.

In my experience, smart women give themselves the luxury of responding in a considered manner. They pause, buy time if required and put together a comeback that will create a win-win outcome. They don't indulge in highly emotive, base-level 'gut responses' (they leave these for the angry men).

If you'd like to assess yourself using Lois Frankel's *Nice Girls Don't Get the Corner Office* criteria, you can complete the self-assessment here: drloisfrankel.com/corner-assess.

LITTLE GIRL HANGOVER

As I've mentioned, many of our adult behaviours and habits began in childhood, so let's take a closer look at your personal childhood experience and the impact on the development of your courage.

As we develop from little girls into teens, then into adults, we are influenced by many external factors. Some of them have a positive impact on our development, whereas others may be challenging, confronting or even damaging. All of these positive *and* negative things work together to create the microcosm that we grow up within. You might say they create the colour and texture of our lives (whether we like it or not!).

It's important for you to acknowledge these factors and consider their impact on you as an adult woman. Here are some examples to stimulate your memory:

- friendships
- spirituality/religion
- physical health
- mental health
- social status
- education
- role models
- money
- media
- celebrities
- social media
- puberty
- body image
- family dynamics
- sexual preference
- intimate relationships
- physical environment
- political climate
- trauma and loss
- genetics.

Journal time

CHILDHOOD INFLUENCES ON THE DEVELOPMENT OF COURAGE

Use the list above as a starting point and spend some time brainstorming all the factors that influenced your development as a little girl. Pay close attention to the things that you believe influenced your behaviours around fear and courage. What insights does this process offer you?

I'm wondering if you have a little girl hangover.

No, I'm not talking about under-age drinking. I'm referring to the childish behaviours that we developed as kids, behaviours that made sense and absolutely served us at that age. These behaviours become 'hangovers' when they are inadvertently dragged into adulthood.

Many of these 'problem behaviours' are perceived as CUTE when you're six, but DYSFUNCTIONAL when you're 36.

Sometimes, when faced with a challenging situation that might bring up fear and vulnerability, adult women can revert back to childish behaviour *rather* than stepping into courage.

I'm going to share seven examples of this type of behaviour with you and I'd like you to be truly honest with yourself here. Consider each one and think about whether this type of childish behaviour has a tendency of showing up in your adult life.

Remember: This is *not* about being harsh or blaming yourself for having a little girl hangover; it's simply an exercise in building self-awareness so you can consciously choose to make changes.

BRATTY REACTIVITY

This is throwing a tantrum when you don't get your way. It may take the form of losing your cool or having a hole in your filter, resulting in a loss of control with how you react. We talked about the difference between reacting and responding earlier – this type of behaviour falls into the reaction category. It's quick, quite automatic, ill-considered and immature. You might say things without thinking, raise your voice, show more emotion than you intend and wind up with regrets.

When you demonstrate bratty reactivity you communicate that you are caught up in your own emotions, have little self-control and have low capacity to cope with a challenge.

SULKING

Here you withdraw verbal communication, but visually demonstrate that you are experiencing negative emotions in response to a situation. This is a classic passive-aggressive strategy and often includes contradictory behaviours such as saying 'I'm fine' when you are not, slamming doors, avoiding eye contact and withdrawing from social interaction (while simultaneously demonstrating strong non-verbal signs that you are unhappy).

When you engage in sulking, you communicate that you have underdeveloped communication skills and an immature response to conflict.

INAPPROPRIATE GIGGLING

This is responding to a serious situation with giggling. It can be extremely awkward and self-undermining! Ever burst into giggles at a funeral or in response to someone sharing sad or serious news? Although rarely intentional, it's a behaviour that can come across as disrespectful and insulting to others.

When you inappropriately giggle, you not only offend others but also communicate that you do not have the coping skills or emotional maturity to deal with a serious situation.

PUSHING BUTTONS

Here, you figure out someone's hot buttons (AKA vulnerabilities) and choose to trigger them to get a reaction. Classic *Mean Girls* fare. While most of the little girl hangover behaviours tend to be unconscious or habitual, this one can be more of a strategic decision.

When you push buttons you demonstrate a calculated, mean-spirited attempt to undermine someone else's confidence.

CLINGINESS

Clinginess is being overly dependent on someone, emotionally and physically. This can be the outcome of a poorly formed attachment to parents during childhood or dysfunctional adult relationships. It is characterised by poor boundaries and a tendency to subjugate your needs for those of another.

When you behave in a clingy manner, you communicate to others that they are more important than yourself, that your needs are secondary and that your independence is low.

LITTLE GIRL VOICE

This is when you either consciously or unconsciously adapt your vocal quality to sound more like a little girl than a woman. Sometimes called 'baby talk', it can be a highly manipulative tool to incite the sympathy of others and to get your way. This behaviour essentially puts you in a secondary or child-like role, facilitating a more sympathetic response from others. Some women use this technique with their male intimate partners, perhaps based on its success with their father as a child; clearly this is problematic on a number of levels.

Using little girl voice can seriously undermine your credibility by communicating that your influencing and negotiating skills are under-developed and you lack the capacity to meet an issue head-on.

APOLOGETIC SPEECH

This occurs by over-using the word 'sorry' and constantly seeking permission or affirmation from others. As we previously discussed, this often takes the form of low-assertiveness in conversation and minimises your capacity to be taken seriously.

When you use apologetic speech you are essentially apologising for your existence and giving people reasons not to listen to you or take you seriously.

Journal time

LITTLE GIRL HANGOVER

Draw up this table in your journal and take time to reflect on any examples of these behaviours in your life. Try not to judge yourself too harshly – we all do it!

	Tick	Example of a time I demonstrated this behaviour in adulthood:	The impact on others was:	The impact on the way others perceive me was:
Bratty reactivity				
Sulking				
Inappropriate giggling				
Pushing buttons				
Clinginess				
Little girl voice				
Apologetic speech				
Others				

COURAGE EMERGES WHEN WHAT WE WANT IS BIGGER THAN WHAT WE FEAR

Letting go of little girl behaviours and, indeed, expanding our comfort zones in general require a good dose of courage. While the steps may be quite straightforward or even simple in nature, the very act of confronting, questioning, reframing and changing a well-ingrained pattern of behaviour can be very difficult.

Making the decision to expand your comfort zone can bring up feelings of fear and uncertainty. As we've discussed, we humans *prefer* our lives to stay pretty much the same – we like the stability. So it's perfectly natural to encounter a little fear when contemplating stepping into a bigger life.

This is where having a clear vision for your future becomes a powerful tool. In my experience, the best antidote to fear is desire! Remember the heroes we mentioned back in Chapter 1, such as Anne Frank, Rosa Parks and the frontline health workers helping during the pandemic? They all had or have a higher purpose, a desire to achieve something bigger than themselves. Now, I'm not saying everything you do has to be for a noble cause; it just has to mean something to YOU.

When you can identify WHY a goal is important to you and the value it holds in your life, your motivation to overcome your fears becomes much stronger.

So when you place your fears on one side of the scales and goals on the other, which is heavier?

Journal time

FEAR VS GOALS

Revisit the Courage Balance Sheet activity from Chapter 1 (see p. 31) in your journal. What factors did you identify as the ones you 'feared' and those that you 'wanted' when remembering a situation where you showed courage? How did each measure up?

Now apply that approach to a future activity to help you find your courage. Think of an upcoming situation – something that you need or want to do – in your life that is already inducing fear.

Create two columns in your journal with the headings:

- What I want
- What I fear

Use this as a guide to help you tease out the things that make you feel fearful and the things that you are working towards. If you found it helpful with the Chapter 1 activity, again give each item on each list an importance rating out of 10 so you can make meaningful comparisons between factors.

THE POWER OF THE FIRST STEP

Taking ONE STEP into the stretchy edges of your expanded comfort zone can quite literally change your life.

I know this sounds dramatic, but I really mean this.

When done intentionally, the first step can change your mindset, your identity and your readiness for bigger shifts.

So, what happens when you take the first step?

Firstly, the internal story you tell yourself changes from:

'I want to write a book' – future focused

to:

'I am writing a book' – present focused.

As we've learned, the stories we tell ourselves create an emotional reality for us. This emotional reality then drives our performance and we start to *become* something new. Once you engage your mindset in this way, you are signalling to your brain that you are already in the process of creating something new.

Next, your personal identity starts to shift. That is, the way you see and define yourself. For instance:

'I am a wannabe author' – future wish

becomes:

'I am an author' – present statement.

This shift in identity is one of the most powerful ingredients in being courageous. When you intentionally start to shift your identity, you take control of the situation at a deep level, connecting with your core values. This is why it is often recommended that you create affirmations in the present tense, with a clear link to your identity. For example, rather than:

'I deserve happiness'

try:

'I am becoming the happiest version of myself.'

Can you feel the difference here?

Journal time

MY FIRST STEP

It's time to take your first step into courage.

Choose an area of your life that you really, deeply want to change. This needs to be something that is important to you, a change that will have a powerful impact on the quality of your life.

In your journal, complete these statements:

- I am (doing) . . . . [the action you want]
- I am (being) . . . . [the identity you want]

Reflect on how it feels to say these statements out loud. How does it impact your posture, your energy, your feeling of confidence?

Next, make a decision about the FIRST STEP you will take towards *becoming* this change. Write about how you are going to move into the stretchy, flexible edges of your comfort zone. Record the thoughts that come up for you, how this feels and what action you are taking.

I'm hoping that these examples of nice girl behaviour, mean girl behaviour, little girl hangover and toxic femininity have helped you to form a good understanding of where your own courageous behaviour needs to sit.

Without being 'too nice' at one extreme or 'toxic' at the other, you'll find your balance somewhere in the middle. Now is your opportunity to think strategically about your personal brand and its intersection with courage:

- Who are you when you are being courageous?
- What do you think, feel and do when being courageous?
- What impact do you have on others?
- What three things can you do to increase your courage?

Now you're ready for the next stage of the C Word Method where you will begin to convert your courage into confidence.

part three

Deep Confidence

FEAR MASTERY

SMART COURAGE

DEEP CONFIDENCE

FLUID COMPETENCE

> Your success will be determined by your
> own confidence and fortitude.
>
> **MICHELLE OBAMA**

I use the term Deep Confidence very intentionally. We've all seen superficial or even false confidence before – it's usually quite fleeting, transparent and not very impressive. I'm here to introduce you to the power and significance of *genuine* self-belief.

Now that you have started mastering fear and are beginning to feel more comfortable in discomfort, I think you're ready to discover the power of Deep Confidence.

Deep Confidence is achieved when your self-esteem and self-efficacy work together to give you an unwavering belief that 'you can do it and you deserve it'. This self-belief is something you can access when you start mastering fear and stepping into Smart Courage. We'll consider how to build confidence from the outside in *and* the inside out and look at ways to rebuild yourself after a crisis of confidence.

Deep Confidence is your key to unlocking the next level of well-being, satisfaction, happiness and success.

DEEP
CONFIDENCE

CHAPTER 7

Yes...

YOU CAN

We've all been guilty of it at some point in our lives. We're not proud of it, we probably wouldn't admit it publicly, but we've felt jealous of another woman.

A more *confident* woman.

You know the type – her life seems effortless. She's from a gifted genetic line of not only beautiful but supremely confident achievers. She is so popular, so alluring, people are simply drawn to her. She has no problem striking up a conversation with anyone and regard-less of their background people just seem to like her. She never looks nervous, even before giving a speech or fronting up to a job interview – she just seems to take it all in her stride. Successful relationships, loads of friends, career mastery and a great butt . . . she has it all.

If you're like many woman, you might feel jealous for a moment, then shake it off with justifications like:

- She was born confident, it's her genetics.
- She was brought up by confident parents.
- She has an unfair advantage in life.
- She's lucky.

You might even tell yourself that she has the confidence 'gift' and you don't, so you could never be like her.

Well, I'm calling BS.

Confidence, like all psychological constructs, is a product of both genetics and environment – nature and nurture. Certainly, some people are provided with a predisposition for confidence through their biological heritage or early family experiences. Yes, this may provide them with a leg-up in the confidence stakes but it doesn't necessarily mean they are destined for a happy and successful life.

And similarly, if your genetics or early life experiences seemingly undermine the development of your confidence, you are not destined for a dull, uneventful or mediocre life.

The good news – you have control over your level of confidence!

CONFIDENCE IS A SKILL-SET

Think of confidence as a sport.

You need to learn the basic fundamentals, understand the rules, discover the unwritten rules, become accustomed to the culture, practise the skills, learn the plays, make mistakes, learn lessons, lose and win, commiserate and celebrate.

And like many sports, some people have genetic advantages but more often than not the stand-out performers are the ones who work hard and overcome adversity.

Confidence is a set of skills that relate to your:

- thoughts – holding an optimistic and self-affirming mindset
- feelings – experiencing positive emotions
- actions – taking courageous action
- identity – becoming and being a confident person.

As we all know by now, the function that drives each of the categories of skills above is your **self-talk**.

Essentially, the underlying driver that stops most people from stepping into their confidence is fear.

Here are examples of fear-based confidence excuses:

- 'I'm not ready to lose the weight.' (AKA I'm scared I will fail and my partner will reject me.)
- 'I'd rather not speak up in the meeting.' (AKA I'm scared people will laugh at my ideas and I'll be humiliated.)
- 'I'm playing the field, I don't want to get serious about dating.' (AKA I'm afraid that if I make myself vulnerable, I'll be abandoned.)

These are excuses (or self-sabotaging internal monologues) that stop you from being your best, fulfilling your potential and, dare I say it . . . Living Your Best Life. #blessed

You have a choice over your level of confidence.

Yes, we all have histories, we've experienced pain and lived through adversity. We've had to overcome really tough situations, we've been beaten down, we've been marginalised, discriminated against, we've been abused and undermined. This is not to be minimised. But . . .

You don't become confident in spite of your history.
You become confident because of it.

At some point in life you have to make a choice. Are you going to be a victim of your circumstances or are you going to be the hero of your own story? I figure you've picked up this book for a reason and if my hunch is correct, I believe you are ready to make the right choice.

The choice of confidence.

TYPES OF CONFIDENCE

Confidence is an optimistic belief in your
personal worth and capability.

Confident people tend to have optimistic beliefs; they focus on positive results and are more likely to take calculated risks because they have less fear of the outcomes. Being confident means you are more likely to be proactive in solving problems, more curious about opportunities and more engaged in setting outcome-focused goals.

There is much debate in psychological research about how many different types of confidence exist (ranging from three to 14 depending on which study you read). Let's take a look at four types that are likely to be most relevant to you.

Self-confidence

This type of confidence is our main focus here. This is about having a positive self-image – '*I am a good person*' – and the belief that you are capable, deserving and on track to achieve everything you want in life. Your self-confidence is the set of beliefs you take into your relationships, career, community, every aspect of your lived experience and it guides you through challenges and change.

Confidence in others

You know you have confidence in others when you can readily build trust and you have faith that others can be relied upon. This is essentially the belief that '**Most people are good people**'. Of course, if you've experienced trauma caused by others, this can be a difficult type of confidence to rebuild.

Confidence that change can be a good thing

We all know that change can be scary, but it also represents opportunities for growth. This is about believing that, despite the uncertainty or ambiguity, you have the capacity to work through it and bounce back. This type of confidence is closely linked to your resilience and growth mindset, and is particularly important when you are faced with chaos. It's based on the belief that '**I see the possibilities and I can adapt**'.

Confidence to know it's going to be okay

This can be the toughest type of confidence to build or rebuild. It is closely related to *optimism* – that is, the belief that everything will be okay. Sometimes, when faced with pain, trauma or significant challenge, it takes all your strength to believe that everything will be okay. This is about looking beyond the immediate situation, separating yourself from the strong emotions present and projecting forward with optimism. It's the belief that '**I'll get through this and I will be okay**'.

Journal time

THE FOUR TYPES OF CONFIDENCE

In your journal, reflect back and find a memory that matches each of these beliefs:

- I am a good person.
- Most people are good people.
- I see the possibilities and I can adapt.
- I'll get through this and I will be okay.

Write about the situation that led to you developing each belief. How can each of these beliefs help you to build confidence in your career, relationships and life?

WHAT'S THE BIG DEAL ABOUT CONFIDENCE?

By now, you might be thinking, 'Why are you SO obsessed with confidence, Mel?' And this would be a fair question. I always knew that, from a deeply personal perspective, my confidence was a great enabler in my life. As I grew up, I saw time and time again that when I entered a situation with confidence I generally achieved the results I desired.

But, of course, there is more to this story than just my own experience.

As a social scientist, I'm fascinated by everything to do with humans: our motivations, our interactions and our performance. So let's delve into some of the broader psychological benefits of being confident.

In their 2018 resource *The Self-Confidence Workbook: A Guide to Overcoming Self-Doubt and Improving Self-Esteem*, psychologists Barbara Markway and Celia Ampel list the five psychological benefits of having confidence:[17]

1 Less fear and anxiety

We've talked about reframing and the capacity to recognise, challenge and change our unhelpful thoughts. When you possess self-confidence, you have a greater sense of being 'in control' of your thoughts and are less likely to believe everything your thoughts tell you.

The more confident you become, the more independent you become from your thoughts.

As your confidence grows, so does your capacity to look at a thought as an 'observer' to evaluate the thought and make an informed choice about your reaction – rather than automatically responding in a highly emotive fashion and getting 'sucked in' to anxious thought patterns.

2 Greater motivation

Self-confidence will help you battle Imposter Syndrome head-on. Your motivation to overcome little obstacles (like your negative self-talk) and big ones (like The Patriarchy) will grow, and your capacity to back your desires with smart action will flourish.

If motivation is the doorway to getting what you want in life, then confidence is your KEY.

3 More resilience

A self-confident woman looks at failure and asks 'What can I learn from this?' She understands that failure is just a stepping stone on her path to success; she knows that there is critical data in the details of her failure. Of course, we all fail, but the deeply confident woman finds ways to bounce back with self-reflection, humility, strength and style.

4 Improved relationships

We all know an 'insecure woman' in a relationship with a man. Or at least, that's what society labels her. She may be the one who becomes intensely jealous when her man talks to another woman, or who desperately checks her man's text messages when he's out of the room. Perhaps you've even been her. But a self-confident woman balances these insecurities with a reality check and a nice dose of FIGJAM (F*ck I'm Good, Just Ask Me) and ultimately sees it for what it is: the normal ebbing and flowing of an intimate relationship.

5 Stronger sense of your authentic self

A truly self-confident woman is completely in tune with her core values and deepest strengths (we'll get to these in the next part of this book). Self-awareness is the key to long-term, sustainable confidence and enables you to build a foundation of *authenticity*. I know this word is overused but for our purposes I'm talking about having a deeply honest relationship with yourself, looking squarely in the mirror every day and going through a mental checklist of 'who I am' and 'who I am not'. A strong sense of self includes knowing the parts of yourself that are 'still in development' and those that are 'proudly flourishing' and celebrating both.

Journal time

THE FIVE BENEFITS OF CONFIDENCE

Write the name of each of these psychological benefits at the top of a new page (so, five pages in total):

- Less fear and anxiety
- Greater motivation
- More resilience
- Improved relationships
- Stronger sense of your authentic self

Now, for each benefit, answer the following:

- What would a boost in this area mean for me?
- How would this impact my:
  - relationships
  - career
  - body acceptance
  - potential to achieve my goals?

You don't

become confident

in spite of your
history.

*You become
confident*

BECAUSE OF IT.

OVERCONFIDENCE: ALL FUR COAT, NO KNICKERS

Have you ever met or worked with someone you'd describe as overconfident? You know, someone who's 'all fur coat, no knickers'?

Ever jumped in the car with someone who was overly confident about their navigational skills? 'Oh I don't need a map, trust me, I know the way.' Fifteen minutes into the trip you start to notice that the scenery looks unfamiliar and your driver is becoming a little sheepish. You ask if they need assistance but their overconfidence (you might call it ego) doesn't allow them to take advice nor check the map, so they keep driving, maintaining the charade that they know the way. By about 30 minutes into the trip, your driver finally concedes that he, sorry, they may have taken a wrong turn somewhere and you've wasted half an hour of your life that you will never get back.

Overconfident people sometimes come across as 'cocky' and you might find them a little 'too much' (or 'extra' as some say). You might notice them taking unnecessary risks or putting themselves out there before they are ready.

You could say that their subjective belief about their capability is greater than their objective competence to deliver.

One of the more socially frustrating traits that overconfident people share is the tendency to 'brag' or 'boast' or 'big themselves up'. Most people find this quite annoying because, at its core, it's about making big claims without always having the capacity to deliver. It's about overestimating oneself and (especially within Australian and British culture) this does not go down well.

Typically, when people brag and fail to follow through, we see them as lacking substance – and this is a sure-fire way to reduce credibility. One of the underlying features of positive relationships is TRUST and when people overshoot the mark on their own capabilities, we lose trust in them. We start to doubt their capacity to deliver on their promises and even start to doubt the honesty of their communication. We start to ask ourselves, 'Is everything they say exaggerated? Are they really as good as they say they are?' and even check back through our memory for other evidence of exaggerated strengths. We lose faith in their ability to be who and what they say they are, which is essentially their integrity.

Overconfidence often develops when someone bases their belief about their potential on their own preconceived notions of their ability, rather than their actual performance. This is often reinforced throughout their life when they succeed and fail. When they succeed, they tend to attribute the positive results to their innate abilities and when they fail, they might blame external forces. This often leads to a lack of personal insight and an inaccurate understanding of one's own weaknesses.

People with overdeveloped confidence tend to:

- take on too much
- stretch beyond their capabilities
- be overly optimistic (AKA Pollyanna)
- burn out quickly
- up-sell themselves.

Overconfidence can alienate others, diminish rapport and undermine social connections.

Overconfidence = not a good look.

A HIGH-PROFILE CASE STUDY IN OVERCONFIDENCE: ELIZABETH HOLMES, CON (WO)MAN

Now might be an opportune moment to admit to my dirty little secret.

I'm a scam junkie.

That's right. I'm obsessed with learning everything I can about overconfident people – traditionally called con men, which interestingly is short for 'confidence men'. Books, documentaries, podcasts, I devour them all. Some people are into true crime, others geek out on the supernatural. For me? It's all about unpacking how these clever and often pathological people get away with tricking and manipulating people, and, sometimes, literally getting away with murder.

From paedophile Jeffrey Epstein to serial abuser and rapist Jimmy Savile, I'm fascinated by high-profile people who live double lives and I'm fixated on understanding *how* they operate. Like Leonardo DiCaprio's character in the movie *Catch Me If You Can,* they capitalise on their overconfidence to disarm others, heavily influence them and ultimately abuse their trust and create massive damage. Not particularly uplifting recreational reading, I know, but hey, we all have our quirks. #nojudgment

Until recently, most of my scam fascination centred around the behaviour of men. This was unsurprising to me as, to generalise, the male brain tends to be more geared towards risky, highly competitive and dangerous behaviour. And to continue the generalisation, women tend to have more empathy and compassion and they find it more challenging to actively deceive.

And then I discovered Elizabeth.

Elizabeth Holmes dropped out of Stanford University in 2004 at the age of 19 to start the blood-testing startup Theranos and grew the company to a valuation of US$9 billion. She became the world's youngest self-made billionaire.

People described her as the 'female Steve Jobs' and, fascinatingly, she embraced this by adopting Jobs' signature style of the black turtleneck uniform. She changed her voice from what was described as a 'normal female voice' at university to a deep, masculine tone as a businesswoman in a male-dominated world (strangely, she would fall back into her natural, more feminine voice after a few drinks!).

She and her company claimed that they could test for a range of different medical conditions based on only a tiny sample of blood taken from a finger pinprick. Holmes said the tests would be able to detect medical conditions like cancer and high cholesterol in an instant.

Obviously, this was seen as revolutionary technology that would overhaul the arduous, slow and painful process of traditional blood testing. Holmes' invention and her passionately persuasive communication style were so impressive that she managed to secure US$70 million in seed funding and the support of highly influential members of the business, political and academic communities.

She would invite high-profile visitors into her lab and test their blood on the spot (but it would later be revealed that the computer monitors were playing video footage of previously recorded dummy data and her team would quickly take the samples out the back and test them on Siemens machines, their direct competitor, using traditional testing methods).

She would speak at prestigious medical and tech conferences, boldly claiming to be changing the face of the global health industry. And the world ate it up.

But it all came crashing down when the shortcomings and inaccuracies of the company's technology were exposed, and Theranos and Holmes were charged with 'massive fraud'.[18] In early 2022, she was found guilty of fraud and conspiracy and could possibly face up to 20 years in jail.

So, what can we learn from the likes of Elizabeth Holmes?

I believe, by examining her overly confident, extreme and toxic behavioural patterns, we get a very real sense of what it looks like when we overshoot the mark with our self-belief.

This story shows us that confidence without humility and integrity can be dangerous weapons.

Now, what happens when we undershoot that mark?

UNDERCONFIDENCE: NO GUTS, NO GLORY

If you imagine confidence as a sliding scale across a continuum, overconfidence is at one extreme and underconfidence, the other. Like all extreme behaviours, neither is good for you. Where the overconfident person might take over the car navigation (despite their skill gap), the underconfident person would likely avoid responsibility for map-reading altogether (quietly expecting themselves to fail and make a fool of themselves).

If the overconfident person tends to dominate the game of life, you might say the underconfident person does not even enter the arena.

Where the overconfident person might be on the top of your 'most annoying people list', the underconfident person might fly under your radar. You might not even notice them (and this is fine by them). People with low confidence tend to avoid risks and stay in the safe lane; they prefer not to put themselves 'out there' or to bring unnecessary attention to themselves.

One of the most difficult aspects of underconfidence is the tendency towards pessimism. Underconfident people tend to expect the worst-case scenario (and, as we know, this can become a self-fulfilling prophecy). This can have a strong, detrimental impact on their life and their capacity to move forward. It's difficult for underconfident people to make their mark on the world as they are constantly playing themselves down, minimising their achievements and avoiding opportunities to shine. Due to their lower tendency to self-promote, underconfident people tend to be overlooked for opportunities in their careers and relationships – others rarely even realise they are interested.

People with underdeveloped confidence tend to:

- avoid risk
- remain in their zone of safety
- be resistant to change
- be pessimistic
- downplay their strengths and achievements.

A HIGH-PROFILE CASE STUDY IN UNDERCONFIDENCE

Um, well, this is a bit awkward.

When I attempted to research all the *high-profile* people with *low levels of confidence* I discovered something very interesting. There are none.

I challenge you to name a highly accomplished person in the public eye who genuinely has poor self-confidence – that is, low self-esteem and low self-efficacy (more on these definitions soon). I'll tell you why you won't find them: their pessimism, lack of belief in their own capability and low motivation to take risks mean that they will not choose to put themselves in what they might perceive as 'risky' situations. And, as we know, to rise above mediocrity and make a name for yourself in your chosen field, you need to challenge yourself to grow, be vulnerable, take risks and push yourself beyond your perceived limits. People with low confidence typically avoid such situations.

However, what I did discover is that there are numerous successful, accomplished, high-profile people out there who overcame circum-stances that didn't support self-confidence in order to achieve their goals and, in the process, make a name for themselves. Such people may have faced early childhood adversity, poor health or genetic deficiencies, yet they found a way to build their confidence and rise above.

Despite circumstances that don't encourage confidence, these legends found the courage to become confident and make a difference.

Mahatma Gandhi (1869–1948)

At the time of Gandhi's birth, India was ruled by England; by the time of his death, India was an independent country, thanks to an independence movement led by Gandhi. As a child he was shy, passive and afraid of the dark and public speaking.

Yet, he grew up to make an indelible mark on the lives of millions of people through his compassionate, values-based activism.

Gandhi led peaceful protests for people who were oppressed, based on his belief of non-violence. He was arrested and imprisoned numerous times for his political beliefs. He published the Declaration of Independence of India and, in a large part because of Gandhi's efforts, India gained independence from England in 1947.

Eleanor Roosevelt (1884–1962)

Roosevelt was a member of the prominent American Roosevelt and Livingston families and a niece of President Theodore Roosevelt. She had a tragic childhood, having suffered the deaths of both parents and one of her brothers by the time she was ten.

Yet, she grew up to become an inspirational female leader and drove positive social and political change for women and the disadvantaged. She also married Franklin D. Roosevelt when she was 21. (Side note: he was, in fact her fifth cousin but it was 1905 and things were 'different' in high society then.)

In 1945 Eleanor was named as the U.S. Delegate to the United Nations. She chaired the committee that wrote the Universal Declaration of Human Rights in 1948. And in 1961 she was appointed by President John F. Kennedy as the chair of the Commission on the Status of Women.

Helen Keller (1880–1968)

Helen Keller had perfect sight and hearing until, at the age of one, she became ill with what was most likely either scarlet fever or meningitis. Once she'd recovered, she could no longer see or hear at all. She didn't learn language until she was around seven, yet at 16 she entered the Cambridge School for Young Ladies, and went on to graduate with honours from Radcliffe College at 24 – the very first deaf and blind person to earn a bachelor's degree in America.

She became a world-famous author and speaker, travelling the world to campaign for the rights of people with disabilities, as well as for civil rights, labour rights and women's rights. She was a founding member of the American Civil Liberties Union. In 1964 President Johnson awarded Keller the Presidential Medal of Freedom and in 1971 she was elected to the National Women's Hall of Fame.

So what's the message here?

Underconfidence is unlikely to set you up for a happy and successful life *but* if you can overcome your self-doubts and work towards something bigger than yourself, there are no limits to what you can achieve.

INTROVERSION: A CAUTIONARY TALE

Before we delve any deeper into our exploration of confidence, I need to dispel a myth.

Underconfidence is not the same as introversion.

Many introverts are confident people and introversion is not about lack of confidence; rather, it is about being more focused on one's thoughts and feelings, as opposed to the outside world.

An introverted person might not actively seek out large social interactions, tending to opt for one-on-one or small group scenarios. This is a reflection of their preference and choice, not their capability. They could step into a bustling social dynamic if and when they actually wanted to, but would probably find it quite demanding and socially draining.

People often make the mistake of assuming that an introverted person lacks confidence – this is not necessarily the case. In fact, some of the most successful, self-confident people have introverted personality styles.

Think:

- Hilary Clinton
- Richard Branson
- Mark Zuckerberg
- Meryl Streep
- Barack Obama
- JK Rowling.

Marissa Mayer was the high achieving and controversial president and CEO of Yahoo! between 2012 and 2016. Despite being a woman in the highly competitive, male-dominated world of big tech, Mayer believed in '*quiet leadership*' and has said, 'I'm just geeky and shy and I like to code'.[19]

At university, Mayer was described as 'hard working and not much for socialising' and when she graduated she had 12 job offers. She decided to go with a fledgling startup called Google, which had less than 20 employees at the time. During her 13-year tenure at Google she briefly dated the company founder, Larry Page, and the pair were described as 'two quiet people dating each other quietly'.[20]

Mayer was credited with the success of Google's search engine as well as products such as Gmail, Google Maps and Google News. When the company went public in 2004, she became rich in an instant. Not bad for a shy girl who liked to code.

There is no doubt that Mayer is a confident woman (it would be close to impossible to achieve these results with an underconfident mindset); she just prefers coding to people.

Journal time

MAP YOUR OWN CONFIDENCE LEVEL

Now that you have sampled the two extremes of confidence (overconfidence and underconfidence) it's time for some self-reflection.

Imagine a confidence continuum from 1 to 10.

UNDERCONFIDENT								OVERCONFIDENT	
1	2	3	4	5	6	7	8	9	10

If underconfidence sits at the bottom of the scale, between 1 and 3 and overconfidence sits at the opposite end, between 8 and 10, where would you plot yourself?

- Why did you choose this number?
- What evidence supports this number for you?
- How do you feel about this number?
- Would you like to shift yourself along the scale? In which direction? Why?
- What three things could you do to move yourself along the scale?

1. Do one thing every day outside my comfort zone
2. Find a mentor / coach
3. Study / Read

DEEP
CONFIDENCE

CHAPTER 8

TWO WAYS TO BUILD CONFIDENCE

(spoiler alert: only one truly works)

In this chapter, we're going to delve into two ways to build confidence – from the inside out and the outside in. While one of these is the ticket to living an authentic, sustainable, confident life, the other plays more of a supporting role (and is not to be mistaken for the main event). But before we do, I'd like to take a closer look at the confidence continuum and help you figure out where you should ideally sit.

THE IDEAL PLACE TO SIT

I wonder where you placed yourself on the confidence continuum.

You've probably figured out by now that Deep Confidence, as a psychological construct, is not necessarily a 'the more the better' situation. Unlike other personality traits (such as friendliness or likeability), a score of 10 out of 10 is not the best scenario for you or the people you orbit.

In my experience, sitting at confidence levels between 5 and 8 will give you the best personal experience and life outcomes.

UNDERCONFIDENT   **OVERCONFIDENT**

| 1 | 2 | 3 | 4 | 5 | 6 | 7 | 8 | 9 | 10 |

IDEAL CONFIDENCE LEVELS

That is, average to above-average confidence is ideal.

As we learned in the previous chapter, overconfidence and under-confidence can become forms of self-sabotage. This is why self-awareness and consistent self-monitoring are so important. If you are currently sitting in the extreme zones, what do you need to do to change this?

I'm going to set you a two-week challenge called the Confidence Audit. I've used this technique with many clients and have found it to be an incredibly effective way to move you along the C Word Method steps – from Smart Courage to Deep Confidence. It's a self-monitoring and self-management activity that enables you to take a close look at yourself, make adjustments and set your confidence dial to the right level for you. But first, let me share with you Carmella's experience.

SPOTLIGHT ON CARMELLA | THE CONFIDENCE AUDIT

Camella and James were in a great relationship. She had a high-powered job as a sales executive in a pharmaceutical company and was kicking serious career goals. She loved going to the gym and quietly smiled to herself each time she lifted heavier or ran faster than the other women in her group. Her friendship group was expansive; as a 'big personality', Carmella seemed to know everyone. And everyone knew her.

On first impression, most people liked Carmella. They were drawn to her effortless charisma and outgoing nature. She knew how to work her network and had that knack of making people feel like they were the only person in the room. With her loud, raucous laugh and tendency to draw attention to herself, Carmella was 'a lot'.

Many people described her as overconfident.

During our time together, Carmella shared with me that she felt 'off' but couldn't put her finger on what was wrong. She said that no one in her life would know anything was different – she was still being her 'typical, big self' – but deep inside, she didn't feel right.

The Confidence Audit

One of the activities we did together was the Confidence Audit. The first week of the activity involved Carmella paying close attention to her confidence highs and lows each day. She set several daily reminders in her phone to prompt her to stop and ask 'on a scale of 1 to 10, how confident am I right now?' At the end of the week, she brought her notes in to discuss with me.

We mapped out her confidence journey for the week on my whiteboard.

Most of her week was spent in the 6 to 8 zone, which was not surprising. But there were clear moments when she spiked at 9 and 10 on her confidence scale. I asked her to describe the *situations* that prompted the extremely high scores. They were:

- talking to her friend at work about their child's birthday
- booking a holiday with her extended family
- discussing maternity leave with one of her team members
- talking to James about the next property they wanted to buy
- having sex with James.

Then I asked her to tap into the emotions she felt in each of these situations:

- bored
- stressed
- judgmental
- frustrated
- stressed.

Now this was interesting. Carmella had identified these moments as 'high confidence', yet the emotions attached were mostly negative.

Something didn't add up.

I asked her to try to remember her self-talk during each of these situations and she reported:

- 'Why do people have to go on and on about their kids?'
- 'Oh great, they'll all ask me the inevitable questions about when we're starting a family.'

- 'She is so happy about becoming a mum, I wish she'd stop gushing.'
- 'If we're talking so easily about real estate, why can't we talk about the baby elephant in the room?'
- 'What's the point in having sex if we can't have a baby?'

We discussed this incongruence and, after a while, I asked Carmella to have another go at defining the emotions she felt in these situations:

- jealous
- stressed
- inadequate
- scared
- scared.

Carmella had tears rolling down her face as she identified these *real* emotions.

Then she went back and recalibrated her confidence scores for these situations. They all sat between two and four. We spent some time unpacking what was going on for her.

Carmella realised that many of the times she went into 'high confidence mode' were probably an overcompensation for feeling desperately sad and scared about her future as a mother. When she and James got together six years ago, he'd made it clear that he didn't want children. At the time, she agreed and they went about their business, building a big life that didn't include children. But now that she was about to turn 40, she couldn't stop thinking about her fertility (and had a private cry each time her period arrived).

This was the first time Carmella had allowed herself to admit that she wanted to become a mother. She shared that she felt desperately scared to talk to James about her change of heart; she felt like she was breaking an unspoken contract between them, like she was betraying him.

The aftermath

Carmella went home and had the difficult conversation with her partner. It was confronting, it was awkward and it was highly charged. They fought, cried and took some time apart.

Eventually, they came together in a more honest place, sharing their authentic hopes and dreams for the future. Carmella openly stated that she wanted to become a mother and James finally admitted that there was a part of him that wanted to be a father too. There was hope.

Last time I saw Carmella, she and James had started the IVF process together.

The lesson I personally learned from Carmella's experience was that confidence is not always as it seems. Even to ourselves. I discovered that confidence has an 'outward projection' and 'inward projection' and the two don't always connect.

THE CONFIDENCE AUDIT

Shifting it up a gear

If you gave yourself a rating on the confidence continuum of between 1 and 4, it might be time to start thinking about boosting your confidence (fortunately for you, you're in the right place!).

But how?

Try this two-week confidence challenge.

WEEK 1

1. **Start with self-awareness** – Spend a week in self-assessment mode. Set reminders in your phone to check in on your confidence levels several times each day (use the confidence continuum to give yourself a quick score out of 10). Record your reflections in your journal each night. What patterns do you

notice? Are your confidence levels higher or lower at certain times of the day? Do particular situations or people trigger changes in your confidence levels?

2. **Observe your impact** – Pay attention to the times when your confidence levels were particularly low. How did others respond to you when you were in this mode? What did you notice about your *impact*? What types of things did people say and do in response to you? How would you describe your capacity to engage with and influence others when in this lower state of confidence?

3. **Master your fear** – Reflect on your lower confidence points throughout the week. Can you identify any specific fears or unhelpful self-talk patterns that were in play at the time? Notice if there are triggers within your environment that caused a fear response for you – could you change anything here?

4. **Activate Smart Courage** – Can you identify any missed opportunities to demonstrate courage? Were there any situations where you opted to avoid taking a risk or deferred to others when you could have stepped up? Were you choosing safer options when you could have taken a little more control of a situation?

Once you have gathered this personal intel (remember, no judgment – it's all data), you'll be in a strong position to start making changes that will move the dial towards greater confidence.

WEEK 2

- **Plan courageous action** – At the start of your second week, set yourself some specific stretch goals. Choose *three situations* where you can demonstrate a little more courage and confidence than last week. Be really specific: write down what you plan to do and how you *predict* this will change the outcome for yourself and the impact on others. Record all your observations in your journal. Continue recording your confidence levels each day and notice what happens to your scores.

Toning it down a little

If you gave yourself a rating of 9 or 10, it might be time to reflect on whether this is serving you.

But how?

Try this two-week confidence challenge.

WEEK 1

1. **Start with self-awareness** – Spend a week in self-assessment mode. Set reminders in your phone to check in on your confidence levels several times each day (use the confidence continuum to give yourself a quick score out of 10). Record your reflections in your journal each night. What patterns do you notice? Are your confidence levels higher or lower at certain times of the day? Do particular situations or people trigger changes in your confidence levels?

2. **Observe your impact** – Pay attention to the times when your confidence levels were particularly high. How did others respond to you when you were in this mode? What did you notice about your *impact*? What types of things did people say and do in response to you? How would you describe your capacity to engage with and influence others when in this high state of confidence? Reflect on Carmella's case study and ask yourself, 'Are my high-confidence moments genuinely high confidence?'

3. **Soften your approach** – Reflect on your highest confidence points throughout the week. Was there objective evidence to support your confidence level (that is, was it valid)? What was the *cost* of being overconfident in these situations? Make sure you're totally honest with yourself here – take the blinkers off. Consider how you could have softened your style this week – what could you have *told yourself* (internal monologue) that would have led to a more humble and engaging impact? What different *words* could you have used with others that would have been more inclusive and less direct? What *behaviours* could have been modified to ensure a higher level of connection and engagement with others?

Once you have gathered this personal intel (remember, no judgment – it's all data), you'll be in a strong position to start making changes that will move the dial towards a more moderate level of confidence.

WEEK 2

- **Plan considered action** – At the start of your second week, set yourself some specific stretch goals. Choose *three situations* where you can demonstrate a more cautious and considered approach. Get really clear about what you'll need to do differently (in your thoughts, feelings and behaviours) to moderate your level of confidence and the subsequent impact on others. Be really specific: write down what you plan to do and how you *predict* this will change the outcome for yourself and the impact on others. Record all your observations in your journal. Continue recording your confidence levels each day and notice what happens to your scores.

THE MOVEABLE FEAST

Most people find that their confidence levels shift from day to day, situation to situation. Confidence is not a static experience; it's dynamic and highly responsive to both internal and external influences.

Internal factors that may influence your confidence levels include:

- amount of sleep
- hormones
- hunger
- mood
- self-talk
- cognitive dissonance (internal conflict or lying to yourself)
- body image.

You may have additional ones to add. Of course, when you run your eyes over this list you'll immediately realise that factors such as these can be highly variable (sometimes, even hard to keep up with).

And some external factors include:

- social dynamics
- weather
- physical comfort levels (such as an uncomfortable wedgie or overly heated room)
- power imbalance
- world news (such as the pandemic or a war).

I'm sure you can add more to the list. And, as you can see, these factors can rapidly change too.

The purpose of developing Deep Confidence is to stabilise your confidence levels and reduce the amount of changeability.

Journal time

CONFIDENCE AND LIFE AREAS

It's not uncommon for women to feel highly confident in one area, say career, while simultaneously lacking confidence in another, such as dating. Take some time to reflect on each area of your life, then give yourself a score on the confidence continuum for each one in your journal (feel free to add other areas that are relevant to you too):

- career
- relationships
- finance
- health and fitness
- body image
- fertility and motherhood
- style
- spirituality
- friendships
- family
- legacy.

UNDERCONFIDENT   **OVERCONFIDENT**

1	2	3	4	5	6	7	8	9	10

I'll bet you don't have a consistent score across every life area.

Very few people do. This is completely normal and there is nothing wrong with having higher levels of confidence in some life areas than others. The key here, once again, is self-awareness. Self-knowledge gives you power – when you are aware of your potential vulnerabilities, you can take conscious and strategic action to manage risks and set yourself up for success.

Next, reflect on these questions for each life area and record your thoughts in your journal:

- Does this score surprise you?
- How do you feel about it?
- What does having this confidence level in this life area mean for you? What is the impact?
- Are you motivated to become more or less confident in this area? Why?
- What three things can you do to change your confidence level in this area?

CONFIDENCE FROM THE OUTSIDE IN

Don't fake it till you make it. Fake it till you become it.
— AMY CUDDY

Scenario 1: She entered the rear of the noisy auditorium. 'Oh, brilliant,' she thought, 'a full house!' Looking up, she saw hundreds of people in the audience – waiting for her. This gave her a tiny shiver of delight and sent excited energy throughout her body. She felt ready and poised for this. She smiled, threw her shoulders back, tilted her chin up and started the long walk towards the stage. As she marched through the crowd making eye contact with as many people as possible, her spiked stilettos clacked, her hips swayed and she felt a thrill as her leather pencil skirt hugged her body. She knew her electric-pink blouse and pussy-bow gave her strength a feminine edge. Her red nails, professionally messy blow-wave and expert make-up were on point and her earrings sparkled. Both men and women in the audience watched her in awe, falling silent and anticipating the energy and charisma she would bring to the stage. They couldn't take their eyes off her. She clearly owned the room and they could not wait to hear what she had to say.

Scenario 2: She cautiously opened the door, just a crack, and peaked into the massive, loud intimidating auditorium. 'Oh sh*t!' she thought, 'So many people, why did I agree to do this?' The idea that all these people were here to hear her speak made her feel physically sick. She wanted to escape but knew she had no choice. As she opened the door and stepped into the room, she felt fear and doubt surging through her body. She wanted to make herself invisible – she wasn't ready. With hands in her pockets and peering at her feet, she took the first tentative steps into the crowd. Her grey trousers and white T-shirt helped her blend in and her flat, comfortable shoes allowed her to walk without sound. Avoiding eye contact, she smoothed her hair to make sure her tight bun was in place and moved towards the stage. Very few members of the audience noticed her presence until she stepped onto the stage and tapped on the microphone.

●

What's the first difference you noticed between these two women?

If you were to rate each woman's confidence out of 10, how would they each fare? And what if you were to predict the success of the impending keynote presentation out of 10?

I'm guessing you probably *believe* that the confident, impactful, charismatic, energetic woman the first scenario is tipped to make a better presentation than the underconfident, cautious, nervous, apprehensive woman in the second. Am I right?

Well, you may be correct. But you may not be.

What if I told you that this happened next?

The woman in the first scenario stepped up to the microphone and shared a bunch of rambling, unrelated ego-driven stories; showed little insight, relevance or intelligence; made arrogant assumptions; and overlooked the opportunity to check in with her audience. Her audience rated her presentation 3 out of 10.

And then, what if I told you that the woman in the second scenario plucked up the courage to nail her presentation? She took a beat to warm up but once she hit her straps she shared fascinating stories, offered imaginative insights, asked her audience to think in a new way and invited their input. Her audience rated her presentation 8 out of 10.

First impressions are not always correct, fair or even rational.

But first impressions do count. You've probably heard of the Halo Effect, which occurs when your first positive judgment about someone unconsciously influences your perception of them as a whole.

The Halo Effect is a cognitive bias (or short-cut) and when applied to confidence it works like this:

- You *appear* to be a confident person.
- People *believe* you are a confident person.
- People *expect* you to have a range of other positive attributes.
- They *respond* to you with positive expectancy, encouragement and support.
- This *reinforces* your feelings of confidence and belief in yourself.

And of course, the opposite is often true too. If you make an under-whelming initial impression, people unconsciously apply the Horns Effect and make assumptions about your below-par competence.

DOES THIS MEAN YOU SHOULD 'FAKE IT TILL YOU MAKE IT'?

Not exactly.

Amy Cuddy is a social psychologist from Harvard Business School I have been following for years. Her groundbreaking 2012 TEDGlobal Talk 'Your body language shapes who you are' taught us that presenting our bodies in a certain way can have an impact on our internal experience of confidence, assertiveness and authority. Cuddy introduced the world to the concept of 'power posing', and her research suggested that we really can build confidence from the outside in.

Cuddy's research found that if you stood in a *high-power* pose, your body increased its testosterone level and decreased its cortisol level, so you had more of the 'assertiveness' hormone and less of the 'stress' hormone. For Cuddy, this change in hormones reflected an increase in feelings of power and confidence.

Her findings suggest that we could literally feel more confident on the INSIDE by making changes to our OUTSIDE.

In her research, she refers to 'expansive' (or high-power) poses and 'contractive' (or low-power) poses. Here are some examples so you can think about them in relation to your own behaviour.

Expansive poses (making yourself bigger) include:

- **Wonder Woman** – Place your feet wider than hip-width apart, with your hands on hips, chest puffed out, chin slightly upward, eyes up. Shift your pose to make yourself appear bigger. This can take you from looking meek to seeming assertive.
- **Tall and Proud** – Take a private moment to lift your chin and hold your arms up in a V-shape, like you've just won a race. This can make you seem (and feel) more powerful.

Contractive poses (making yourself smaller) include:

- **Protective** – Placing your hands on your face or neck, which is a low-power pose that communicates the need for protection from others.
- **Hand-hiding** – Hiding your hands in your pockets is another low-power pose and it hints that you may lack self-confidence.

Like many of the tall poppies I mention, Cuddy and her research have been harshly criticised. Others have attempted to replicate the hormonal changes in her research and found the link between power posing and her reported effects to be at best weak and, at worst, a farce.

A critical analysis of Cuddy's research and other studies on posture effects led to this damaging summary: 'The existing evidence is too weak to . . . advocate for people to engage in power posing to better their lives.'[21]

It appeared the power pose had been debunked.

But then in 2018, Cuddy and her team came back fighting and, after a comprehensive review of another 55 studies, found 'strong evidential value for postural-feedback (i.e., power-posing) effects and particularly robust evidential value for effects on emotional and affective states (e.g., mood and evaluations, attitudes, and feelings about the self)'.[22]

Certainly, Cuddy's 2018 claims are 'softer' than her original findings in 2012, but her premise remains:

We can influence the way we feel on the inside by changing the way we show up on the outside.

Regardless of the debate in the academic world, I have to say I'm a huge personal advocate of the power pose. I have been known to step into a bathroom before going onstage or on camera for a quick two-minute Wonder Woman! Whether it has an impact on my hormone levels may be debatable but I can report that it certainly makes me feel:

- more powerful
- more emotionally prepared
- stronger
- more confident
- like my own superhero.

And, when I feel like this, I tend to engage in positive, self-affirming internal dialogue and tend to take more assertive and forthright action.

I wonder if it's the same for you?

Journal time

MY POWER POSE EXPERIMENT

I'd like you to implement this little experiment in real time, just before you have a real-life, important 'thing' to perform. This may be a work meeting or interview, an exam, an important/ challenging conversation or maybe even a break-up.

This is the 'Mel Schilling X Power Pose' edition and I have adapted it over the years based on feedback from my clients. In addition to the physical posture, I like to add in layers that tap into other senses:

- Take some time to yourself right before a high-stakes situation; choose a quiet, private space (a toilet stall is perfect).
- Stand for **two minutes** in your chosen expansive pose (maybe Wonder Woman or the Big V).

- While standing in your pose:
  - use your earbuds for privacy and listen to a track that makes you feel strong, grounded and powerful
  - smell a scent that makes you feel strong (maybe a perfume you wore when you had a previous success or an aromatherapy oil that invigorates you)
  - perhaps you have a mint or sweet that you suck in preparation for important events – if so, savour the taste as you feel strong and powerful
  - visualise yourself in a winning scenario
  - smile proudly.
- You may not opt to use all of these ideas but try to layer at least one additional sense over the posture.

What happens? Record your experience in your journal.

Even if the effects of the power pose prove to be a function of the placebo effect, does it really matter? I see it this way.

When you perform a power pose with clear intent, two things can happen:

1. You *subjectively feel* more assertive, confident and ready to take on a high-stakes situation.

2. Others *perceive* you as more assertive and confident and, due to the Halo Effect, make positive assumptions about your worth and potential capability.

When these two forces work together, you set yourself up for greater social success.

DO YOU WEAR A POWER SUIT?

Let's take this 'confidence from the outside in' idea one step further. As well as your physical posture, you have a range of other external features that can enhance or inhibit your feelings of confidence.

To the outside world, these features constitute part of your non-verbal communication.

To you, they can form part of your confidence armour. These physical features can be your Power Suit and help you to 'fake it till you become it' as Amy Cuddy says. They include:

- clothing
- grooming
- gestures
- positioning
- speed of movement
- speech patterns.

These non-verbal cues can all work together as part of your overall approach, to help you feel and therefore be more confident.

BUT external factors will only get you so far.

You've heard all the chatter about the negative impact of social media, 'comparisonitis' and the obsession with filters on our self-esteem. If you're feeling crappy about yourself and take a casual scroll through all the 'highlight reels' on Instagram, you will end up feeling worse. Right?

WARNING: A confidence boost from the outside in is only ever temporary and only touches the surface of your psychological health. If you were to focus exclusively on your external appearance of confidence without doing the inner work, you'd miss the opportunity to experience Deep Confidence.

Being overly reliant on your looks, your likes or your locks will be your undoing if confidence is your goal.

CONFIDENCE FROM THE INSIDE OUT

You want to feel that authentic inner confidence but how do you get it? How do you access your psychological resources to become truly confident? You focus on building your C word from the inside out.

Deep Confidence = self-esteem + self-efficacy

Being overly

reliant on

your looks, your
likes or your locks

will be your

undoing if

CONFIDENCE

is your goal.

Self-esteem is quite literally about liking yourself. It means you hold a positive evaluation of yourself and believe that you *deserve* to be happy. **Self-efficacy** is about believing you have the *capability* to master skills and achieve goals, and that you can persevere in the face of setbacks.

The concept of self-esteem is often mistakenly used as a synonym for confidence but, as we're learning, confidence is broader than simply liking yourself. In addition to the positive self-directed feelings, confidence involves the clear belief in your skills, knowledge and attributes.

A confident woman FEELS she deserves positive things and BELIEVES she has what it takes to bring them to fruition.

Let's take a closer look at how self-esteem and self-efficacy differ:

	SELF-ESTEEM	SELF-EFFICACY
SELF-TALK	'I am worthy'	'I am capable'
FOCUS	Present focused	Future focused
SOURCE	Based on emotion	Based on experience
STABILITY	Can be highly changeable	Tends to be more stable

These two psychological constructs have an intimate and dynamic relationship. Self-esteem sits deep inside (think of it like the 90 per cent of an iceberg that's below the surface); it links to our core beliefs about our worthiness and value, and it can shape our entire life experience. Self-esteem can be intrinsically linked to our childhood experiences, the formation of our identity and the way significant people treat us.

Imagine a young girl who is abused by her parents. The very foundation of her self-evaluation becomes disrupted – she misses the chance to build a positive evaluation of herself because everything in her developing world tells her that she is worthless. As she moves into adolescence, she embeds these feelings and starts to tell herself 'I don't deserve to be happy', so she makes choices that put her in harm's way, and being hurt seems to feel normal and right. As an adult, her feelings and beliefs develop into 'I don't deserve love' and she consistently chooses partners who treat her poorly. Her negative self-evaluation becomes the leading player in her life. This is self-esteem and in this instance it's low.

Now imagine the same girl at school. Her negative self-esteem means that when she fails, it feels like a reinforcement of her parents' message. It feels right. She tries to calculate a maths problem, but gets it wrong. Rather than trying again, she gives up telling herself, 'I'm no good with numbers . . . I can't do it.' As she grows up, her negative belief about her ability with numbers becomes a 'fact' to her; she sees it as evidence that she is not capable of managing her money. This becomes the expectation that she will not ever be able to get out of debt, that she does not have the potential for financial independence. This is self-efficacy.

This time, imagine a young girl who is nurtured by her parents. She grows up in a supportive environment and is regularly praised. She is allowed to make mistakes, and learn from them, but is never judged or shamed. Her family encourages her to focus on her strengths and she learns how to put herself in situations that will bring out her best. As she grows up, she builds strong and positive relationships with her friends and sets boundaries to keep herself safe and happy. As an adult, she freely tells herself 'I deserve love' and makes romantic choices that lead her to wonderful relationships. This is self-esteem and in this instance it's high.

Now imagine the same girl at school. Her positive self-esteem means that when she fails, she just sees it as feedback. She gives herself opportunities to try and fail and try again; she is resilient and perseveres until she gets it. Although she doesn't like maths, she sees it as a challenge and knows that mastering this subject will open up a world of possibilities to her in the future. Each time she conquers a little maths problem she celebrates and rewards herself with chocolate. Over time, she starts to believe that she *is* good with numbers (because all her little 'wins' along the way have demonstrated this). She ends up in a flourishing career as a financial adviser and often tells the funny story about how she hated maths as a kid. This is self-efficacy.

THE SYMBIOSIS OF SELF-ESTEEM AND SELF-EFFICACY

As self-esteem is based primarily on *emotions*, it can be a changeable construct. For some women, self-esteem can go up and down depending on their hormones, relationships, the season or amount of sleep they've had. Self-efficacy, however, tends to be based on *evidence* (or at least our perception of the evidence) and therefore can be a more objective and stable construct.

But of course, we are talking about human nature and a deeply personal experience, so no hard-and-fast rules apply. Agreed?

So, how do they play together?

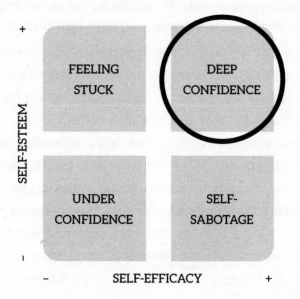

Let's say you have low self-efficacy but high self-esteem. You might believe you are worthy of success but are not sure if you are capable of achieving it. You probably become frustrated at your lack of progress and feel stuck with no real path out of your situation.

What if you have high self-efficacy but low self-esteem? You know you have what it takes, but you doubt yourself. You probably second-guess yourself even though you've done it before and have had good results. This is likely to undermine your capacity to follow through (even though you know what to do). Remember our old friend Imposter Syndrome? This is where she lives.

And what about low self-efficacy and low self-esteem? This is where low confidence sits. Not only do you believe you are not worthy of a happy and successful life, but when you look at your life experience, you can't see any examples of where you have had small wins. This is not a healthy place to be from a mental health perspective.

It is ideal to have high self-efficacy and self-esteem. This essentially means you believe you are worthy and deserving of living a happy and successful life, and you have the chops to make it happen. Your destiny is in your own hands and you're highly motivated to overcome obstacles, persevering to get the ambitious results you know you can achieve.

So, we can see that there are two ways to build confidence:

- from the outside in
- from the inside out.

The only method that will give you long-term, sustainable and stable confidence – Deep Confidence – is the inside out. By building (or rebuilding) a solid foundation of belief in your worthiness and capability, and maintaining this every day, you will be well on your way to a confident life. Yes, using some of the outside-in techniques such as power poses and the Halo Effect will help, but alone they are not enough. In order to step into your potential as a strong woman and to enjoy the feelings and benefits of Deep Confidence, it's critical that you harness your self-talk in a self-compassionate and affirming manner to build a set of psychological resources to lift you up. And when you do, anything is truly possible.

DEEP
CONFIDENCE

CHAPTER 9

Bouncing back

FROM A CRISIS
OF CONFIDENCE

After years of working towards my career goals, something incredible happened when I finally felt that I had *arrived*. Along the journey, I had endured so many setbacks, overcome obstacles, dealt with rejection and humiliation and also experienced the exhilaration of small wins. I had sacrificed my love life for years, lived an unbalanced life (workaholic, anyone?) and poured my heart and soul into my mission to build my business and make a positive impact on the world. So, after two decades of climbing the mountain, I felt like I had reached the peak and . . .

I finally allowed myself to EXHALE.

The sense of accomplishment, pride and satisfaction that come with achieving something BIG is worthy of celebration! But it also brings with it a quiet time of reflection, humility and calm. For me, I have really noticed the calmness that comes with being in 'flow' and I have an almost overwhelming sense of relief ('Ahhh . . . I did it!').

Sometimes, when I'm on a TV set or stage, I steal a private moment of gratitude and take a deep breath – as I exhale, I let myself appreciate the moment and honour myself for getting there. And I smile.

One of the most powerful lessons I have collected from my yoga practice over the years is the value of visualisation, abundance and, most importantly, BREATH. When a teacher guides me through a cycle of breath with suggestions like 'Breathe in love, positivity and strength . . . and breathe out fear, pain and control' I can clearly visualise the negative sentiments leaving my body.

Now, as you know, I'm a behavioural *scientist*. You might be wondering why I'm suddenly talking about yoga when so far, this book has been more western in perspective.

Well, I truly believe that mental health and wellbeing are best supported by a holistic approach.

There is incredible power in an East meets West approach to self-care. I met the love of my life at 39 so, when we knew we wanted a child, we had to go through IVF. I chose to complement this highly medicalised western process with acupuncture, yoga and meditation. For me, this broader approach gave me a sense of balance throughout the process and helped me manage the fear and anxiety that inevitably came up. Although my hubby (AKA Mr Logical) thought the acupuncture was a placebo, this didn't bother me. It worked for me and gave me a greater sense of calm and control during a process that was 100 per cent beyond my control.

The power of breath may be the bridge between eastern and western philosophies on self-care and wellbeing. Both schools of thought draw on the power of intentional breathing to facilitate positive change in our bodies and lives.

The western medicos would say:

> Slow breathing techniques have been found to enhance autonomic, cerebral and psychological flexibility and studies have found links between parasympathetic activity (AKA the 'rest and digest' process), the central nervous system and activities related to psychological wellbeing.[23]

And from an eastern perspective:

> Deep breathing can allow us to experience our true essence. The flow that the steady in and out action of breathing creates stimulates a transformation in the body and mind, purifying and cleansing them so that our true essence shines forth. Circulation is increased, hormonal balance is cultivated, the organs are regenerated and the nervous system is pacified.[24]

Now, back to the exhale.

Emotionally, exhaling after a deep, mindful breath can be incredibly soothing. You can experience a sensation of expelling negativity and just 'letting go'. On a physical level, deep, slow breathing can calm your nervous system and literally slow down your heartbeat.

When you breathe out, you also expel *vapors*. What are vapors, I hear you ask? Here's a definition:

> **VAPOR** [vey-per]
> *noun:* a visible exhalation, as fog, mist, steam, smoke, or noxious gas, diffused through or suspended in the air.[25]

A visible exhalation. Vapors are the physical embodiment of the process of letting go.

I just love this.

THE VAPOR MODEL

I love this so much that I'm using the concept of the vapor to help you embrace some of the characteristics of confidence – I call it the VAPOR Model.

When it comes to reducing the changeability of your confidence levels and working towards a more consistent, even, balanced experience, a model like this will help to anchor you. Of course, you'll still experience the natural ups and downs and the different levels of confidence in various environments, but this will give you something to come back to.

Come back to, and help you reset after a crisis of confidence.

All you have to remember is VAPOR.

V ULNERABILITY

A SSERTIVENESS

P OSITIVE EMOTION

O PTIMISM

R ESILIENCE

Two decades of working with and educating human beings has taught me that these five features typically show up in the lives of deeply confident people. I consider these a set of anchors for confidence, and they can become your touch point for self-monitoring and readjustment. These five anchors are a foundation of the C Word Method's Deep Confidence.

Before we dive into the VAPOR model I have to share something funny. My nanna used to refer to the experience of 'getting the vapors' as a way to describe her anxiety. As kids we found this hilarious, and my mum, sister and I still get the giggles when we talk about it.

In Victorian times, this quaint expression, *getting the vapors*, was used when a delicate flower of a woman sighed, put the back of her hand to her forehead and required a fainting couch (often in response to someone mentioning something, dare I say it, sexual in nature!).

The vapors were actually described as 'a disease of nervous disability in which strange images seem to float hazily before the eyes, or appear as if real'.[26]

Good on you, Nanna.

Now, let's dive into the VAPOR Model and its five features of Deep Confidence.

V FOR VULNERABILITY

Confident women happily demonstrate vulnerability. As Brené Brown says, 'Vulnerability is not winning or losing; it's having the courage to show up and be seen when we have no control over the outcome.'

You can't discuss vulnerability without examining the wonderful work of Brené Brown. She is a research professor at the University of Houston, as well as the author of the number one *New York Times* bestselling book *Daring Greatly: How the Courage to Be Vulnerable Transforms the Way We Live, Love, Parent, and Lead*. Her research on the concept and experience of vulnerability has powerfully changed the conversation about what it means to 'show weakness' in our relationships, careers and life.

Brown's key findings show that vulnerability is the core of shame and fear and our struggle for worthiness, but it's also the birthplace of joy, of creativity, of belonging, of love. As she explains it: 'Vulnerability is basically uncertainty, risk, and emotional exposure . . . Vulnerability is not knowing victory or defeat, it's understanding the necessity of both; it's engaging. It's being all in.'[27]

When we talk about courage as part of the C Word Method, we are talking about vulnerability in action. Emotional risk-taking is the underpinning function of courage and it's impossible to take such risks without making yourself vulnerable.

To show vulnerability is to broadcast to the world 'I'm HUMAN, warts and all, accept me as I am!' It's a way of communicating that you accept your whole self, including your imperfections, and are open to the process of learning and changing. Being vulnerable means acknowledging that you are a work-in-progress and you are okay with that.

One of the brilliant side-effects of showing vulnerability is that it is incredibly *attractive*. This might seem counter-intuitive, especially to those of us who strive for the glossy, Insta-worthy, highly filtered version of existence. But in the real world, people are drawn to others who show their fault lines – it's reassuring and facilitates connection between people. When we see and come to know someone with flaws, it reminds us that it's okay if we have flaws too. It shows us that we are all in this thing called life together – we are all muddling through and no one has it mastered. This feeling fills us with reassurance and permission to be real, to be authentic, to connect.

Showing vulnerability is disarming to others. When you lead with vulnerability, it allows others to quickly drop their guard in response, and this fast-tracks the building of trust.

Being vulnerable means you are willing to forgo a level of power or to diminish your own status in order to allow someone else to take the stage. Vulnerability happens when you find a way to put your ego on hold, if only for a minute.

Here are three simple words you can use to start showing vulnerability today:

Help. Sorry. Thank you.

- Asking for help communicates 'I need assistance'. It tells others that you don't have it all figured out, that you are prepared to learn and that you see them as a source of knowledge. When you ask for help, you are bowing down to another, handing over some power and communicating to them that you want them to step up for you. Asking someone for help tells them that you value their input which can build their self-esteem and, in turn, connect them with you.

- When you apologise you communicate 'I own that mistake'. The simple (but not always easy) act of taking accountability can take the wind out of many an argument. By genuinely saying sorry, you communicate that you are at fault, you are not perfect, you are still learning and you are prepared to change. Apologising means you are willing to do better and this shows maturity and strength.

- The simple utterance of thank you communicates the message 'I appreciate you'. This instantly gives the other person a new level of power and status and shows that you are not too proud to acknowledge them. Thank you shows the other person that they occupy an important role in your life and that you highly value their input, and it encourages them to keep doing what they're doing.

Again, this builds their esteem and builds a deeper bond with you. You might surmise that vulnerability, in behavioural terms, is the opposite of toxic femininity. If you recall the problematic behaviours associated with toxic femininity discussed in Chapter 4, they usually come from a place of fear. If people are passionately frightened about exposing their shame, letting their guard down or showing anything they perceive as weakness, then this fear can often come across as aggression, defensiveness or other ineffective communication devices.

In business, contemporary leadership is moving towards a more *authentic* style. Gone are the days where leaders are revered for scaring the sh*t out of their employees. No one wants to work for a boss who believes they are the messiah, barks orders and hides behind their big desk for fear of showing they don't know it all. Thumping the table does not demonstrate confidence, it only tells the room that you are scared you are going to be exposed and are possibly feeling out of your depth.

> **Today, successful leaders demonstrate what might be described as a more feminine approach, leading with emotional intelligence, transparency and vulnerability.**

Vulnerability is such an integral ingredient and a pivotal starting point in the confidence recipe because it sets the framework for courage. Taking baby steps towards a career goal, asking out the hottie in the coffee shop or travelling overseas solo all require you to step into the unknown, to willingly enter into fear – and this, my friend, is vulnerability in action.

Vulnerability is the first step towards confidence.

A FOR ASSERTIVENESS

Confident women assertively communicate their needs.

Being assertive means asking for your needs to be met. It's about separating the emotion from the situation (as much as possible) and making a clear and dispassionate request. Being assertive means you respect yourself, your values and your goals, and you are prepared to take action to ensure that you get what you need and deserve.

Assertiveness is *not* aggressive. We've all heard the stories about women who dare to ask for their needs to be met, only to be labelled a bitch. The woman who speaks up in a work meeting, who sets boundaries with her mother-in-law or says NO to a man's sexual advances.

Genuine assertiveness does not need to be aggressive as it's grounded in healthy self-esteem. To be assertive you must first believe that:

- your needs matter
- you have the right to communicate them.

Once these beliefs are established, assertiveness becomes a rather straightforward pursuit. Yet, for many of us it's not always easy to 'slip into assertive mode'. Years of programming, habit reinforcement and social conditioning can conspire to keep us out of assertive mode in our everyday lives. Cast your mind back to some of the little girl hangover behaviours we discussed in Chapter 6 – depending on your early family experience, culture and a range of other influences, you may naturally veer more towards a passive approach (such as a little girl voice) or an aggressive approach (such as tantrums). I write more about assertiveness, along with passive and aggressive approaches, in Chapter 12 (p. 259).

Essentially, assertiveness is the outward projection of confidence. The power to say NO and set clear boundaries is often perceived by others as confidence. Of course, we know there is much more to confidence, but, when it comes to pursuing your goals, being the mistress of your destiny and carving out an extraordinary life, assertiveness is one of the most critical tools in your toolkit.

P FOR POSITIVE EMOTION

Confident women experience positive emotions every day.

We've talked about the fight, flight or freeze phenomena in this book. Of course, when drilling down into the fear response and exploring how to step into courage, this is a common physiological feature.

But now we are focusing on confidence so it's time to flip this on its head.

The positive psychology field centres on how we can *flourish*. Barbara L. Fredrickson, a prominent scholar in social psychology, affective science and positive psychology, is leading the way with her broaden-and-build theory. This theory is essentially the opposite of the fight, flight or freeze approach – it describes what happens to our bodies when we experience positive emotions (so, the opposite of fear).

Fredrickson's research suggests that positive emotions such as happiness, joy, curiosity, contentment and anticipation broaden our thinking and awareness and lead us to new thoughts and actions. These then encourage us to have new experiences, create new ideas and form new social bonds. A result of this broadened mindset is a greater range of personal, physical, psychological and social resources that help us survive and thrive.[28]

And, as we know by now, a key feature of confidence is believing in your own psychological resources, such as your ability to cope and succeed.

The broaden-and-build theory proposes that our 'capacity to experience positive emotions may be a fundamental human strength central to the study of human flourishing'.[29] In her research, Fredrickson identified a top ten list of positive emotions:

- hope
- love
- gratitude
- interest
- pride
- inspiration
- joy
- serenity
- amusement
- awe.

How many of these would you experience in a typical day?

Something that works really well for my clients is making the commitment to experience three positive emotions from this list per day. I've listed hope at the top as it's considered to be the most powerful of all positive emotions, especially when linked to specific plans for new possibilities in the future.

Perhaps the cleverest thing about positive emotions is that they can stimulate the flow of happy hormones such as dopamine, serotonin, oxytocin and endorphins, which all help you feel good, sleep better, focus more, stress less and feel more connected – you want these hormones flowing in your body.

It's not hard to grasp the powerful benefits of experiencing positive emotions and their sister hormones on a daily basis. When it comes to your confidence levels, each of these hormones have a part to play and we'll explore more on how to tap into them in Part 4.

O FOR OPTIMISM
Confident women are realistically optimistic.

Although it wasn't reflected in Fredrickson's study, optimism is another one of the strong positive emotions that can boost your confidence. Optimism has been shown to protect the mind from symptoms of depression and reduce overall stress levels.

In general, optimistic people seem to be more satisfied and more successful than those who are pessimistic.

Having an optimistic mindset is clearly linked with the development of confidence. As author and career mentor Bud Bilanich wrote in the leadership publication *Fast Company*:

> Self-confident people are optimistic. They take action, even when they are not sure of the outcome. By facing your fears and acting you become more self-confident and optimistic. You become more self-confident because you dared to act – something that is not always easy. You become more optimistic if you succeed because you have conquered a

personal demon. You become more optimistic even if you fail, because you learn one of the great truths of life – failure is seldom fatal.[30]

Of course, this is not about sailing through life with a 'Pollyanna' view of the world. It's important to engage in what I call **realistic optimism**: a positive mindset with your feet planted firmly on the ground. It's a tricky balance, but if you walk the line between expecting positive outcomes and acknowledging the possible constraints and parameters, you're well on your way to confidence and success. Some people talk about 'expecting the best and preparing for the worst' and this is a good way to characterise realistic optimism. We explored the balance between rational and emotional thinking earlier – this is another example of a balanced thinking style. Here, you draw on the emotional and intuitive side of your mind to create an optimistic vision for the future; and balance this by drawing on the more practical and rational side of your mind to keep your vision grounded in reality.

I personally use a realistic optimism approach in my career. When I'm pitching myself for a big, audacious opportunity, I:

- **Dream big!** I start by imagining the best-case scenario (even if it seems ridiculous). I often ask myself, 'What would I want to do/be if there were no barriers to my success?' This type of 'magical questioning' is a great way to tap into the creative and intuitive part of the brain – sometimes my visions are so outrageous that I wouldn't dare share them with anyone, I hold them close. An example of a big dream: I wanted to leverage my experience in the Australian media industry to launch a media career in the UK.
- **Scenario plan.** As a big dreamer, I've learned over the years that scenario planning can help me keep my feet on the ground (this, and a big dose of reality from my hubby, Mr Practical). It's a simple technique that enables me to imagine a range of possible outcomes,

and to think each one through to its practical conclusion. An example of scenario planning: If my UK dream is possible, how will I manage filming schedule clashes? What kind of visas would my family and I need? How will I deal with publicity across two continents? Who will represent my business in the UK? What will we do with our property in Australia? Will we sell the car? What about school for Maddie?

I find this approach allows my optimism to flourish while also ensuring that I cover my bases from a practical perspective. Using realistic optimism helped me achieve this particular dream: in 2021 I landed my first media gig in the UK. Do you see how realistic optimism could work for you too?

R FOR RESILIENCE

Confident women are resilient.

Resilience refers to your ability to bounce back from challenges and adversity. It's not about being fearless or happy all the time; it's not about being impervious to tough times. It's about having the belief that, no matter how tough things get, you *will* get through it.

Through having resilience, you will feel strong enough to keep trying, to keep persevering despite setbacks.

> **You're not strong in spite of your tough times;**
> **you're strong because of them.**

Dr Neil Ginsburg, a paediatrician and human development expert, outlines seven connected, core components that make up resilience in children. I believe – and I'm sure you'll agree – that these relate to adults as well, so here they are from a C Word Method point of view. (And, wouldn't you know it, Dr Ginsburg loves a good C word too!)

Dr Ginsberg's seven Cs of resilience are:

1. **Competence.** You know how to handle stressful situations effectively.

2. **Confidence.** You believe in your own abilities (your confidence is rooted in competence).

3. **Connection.** If you have close ties to friends, family and your community, you are more likely to have a stronger sense of security and belonging.

4. **Character.** Character comes from knowing your values and living with integrity and empathy. Character gives you a strong sense of self-worth and confidence.

5. **Contribution.** By contributing to the world, you realise that you are helping to make it a better place. This helps you feel more connected and find a sense of purpose, your WHY.

6. **Coping.** You have a broad range of coping skills allowing you to be better prepared to overcome life's challenges.

7. **Control.** You understand that you have internal control and agency and can determine results through your actions and choices. This empowers you and helps you know you'll bounce back from life's challenges.[31]

Try to reflect back on the last time you needed to draw on your own resilience. To what degree did each of the 7 Cs play a part for you?

WHAT HAPPENS IF YOU ACHIEVE YOUR DREAMS . . . BUT DON'T EXHALE?

In fact, what if you reach the top of your own personal mountain and rather than enjoying the sweet, gratifying sense of relief and exhalation . . . you hyperventilate (or get the vapors)?

Now seems like a good time to introduce you to my sister, Beck.

With only 23 months between us, we are very close. Very similar. Very different. One thing we definitely both share is our strong ambition and determination to perform to our highest potential. You might say we can both be a little 'one-eyed' when it comes to our careers. #understatement

Beck started her career as a nurse and quickly moved into a critical care role where she worked one on one with very sick patients in ICU, often on life support. Her gorgeous husband, Calum, became a paramedic and the two of them happily navigated their family life as a nurse and ambo while bringing up three incredible kids, Stella and twins Tessa and April.

Beck got a taste of life as a paramedic through Cal's career and thought, 'I want what he's having.' She was drawn to the thrill of managing a crisis and the adrenaline rush of applying her highly attuned medical skills to save a person's life (just between us, this would scare the hell out of me – as I said, although similar, we are very different). So she set about changing her career trajectory from nurse to paramedic and, before long, started to rise up the ranks. You won't be surprised to learn that she set her sights on one of the top jobs in emergency medicine – mobile intensive care ambulance (MICA) paramedic – and decided that she would become one of the few women to step into this high-pressure role.

What followed was *years* of studying, learning, practising and sacrificing to get herself to the point that she was ready to go through the gruelling panel interview process for the role.

In addition to the *external work* of shifting careers and changing uniforms, Beck went deep and did some fundamental *internal work* too. In preparation for her role as a MICA paramedic, she elevated her knowledge base, upgraded her technical and professional skillset, updated her mindset and fundamentally changed her *identity*.

Everything in her world shifted and she *became* a MICA paramedic – this was who she was 24 hours a day. Family dinners, drinks with the girls, pillow talk with her hubby . . . every conversation came back to her career. Achieving the next rung on her career ladder became her singular focus. Her obsession.

And she achieved it.
And then it all went wrong.

She climbed to the top of her mountain and didn't like the view. It wasn't what she expected, wanted or enjoyed. The reality of her new job and life was very different from her expectations. There was a gaping chasm between her perception and reality and this hit hard.

Not one to turn away from a challenge, Beck soldiered on. She pulled on the uniform each day and played the role she had worked so hard to achieve. Let's get real here, she was *literally* saving people's lives every damn day – she went to work, saved lives, went home and felt . . . wrong. Sure, she still lived for the gratification and adrenaline rush of being the first on the scene of a crisis and taking vulnerable people through the worst day of their life with empathy, skill and compassion. But beyond this, something was missing.

She reached burnout. And then, she reached her tipping point.

Now, one of the incredible things about being a Grown-up Human Woman is that we get to adapt, shift, pivot and change our bloody minds! Yes, we can.

So, Beck set out to re-evaluate her career and life. She took some time out (smart move) and started reconnecting with the things that brought her JOY: her family, her garden and horses. She had been a horse-crazy teenager (something I, as a boy-crazy teenager, could never understand), but she'd let this passion go as she moved into the university years and other priorities took over.

Fast-forward 30-plus years and she's back on the horse!

During her career pause, Beck knew I was writing this book and she asked me a brilliant question:

'How do you rebuild confidence after you've lost it?'

I realised this was not just a question for her, but for all of us. As we all know, confidence is not a static experience. You would have seen with the confidence continuum that confidence ebbs and flows with the changes in our internal and external worlds. As hard as we may try to build up that *confidence consistency muscle*, sometimes life comes along and kicks us in the guts.

So, after a challenging experience or a crisis of confidence, how can you crawl your way back to your pre-crisis confidence levels?

START BY HITTING THE RESET BUTTON

There are four steps I recommend for resetting your sense of self after a crisis. These then lead you back to Smart Courage and Deep Confidence.

1 Self-compassion

Before you can start to rebuild anything, you need to cut yourself some slack. Life happens, things change, some things are beyond your control – give yourself a break! This is no place for harsh self-judgment. Sure, it might be your initial gut reaction, but don't allow this to colour your next chapter. Monitor and challenge your self-talk very closely during this phase, and constantly come back to self-compassion.

You are not Wonder Woman,
you are WonderFUL Woman.

If you can, give yourself the gift of time and space. When we've been through something challenging, difficult or traumatic, one of the best

YOU ARE NOT

Wonder Woman,

YOU ARE

WonderFUL Woman.

things we can do is just STOP. Take time out from everything and everyone that influences you – it's vitally important to find a way to reconnect with your inner world and get in touch with your own deep feelings about the situation. To effectively process the situation, you need the 'right information' and, by right, I mean right for YOU. I'm talking about clarifying your *own perspective*, separate from the input and opinions of others. You might achieve this through meditation, exercise, therapy, gardening, painting – whatever you do that switches off the outside world and enables you to go within.

2 Joy and mindfulness

Next, take a leaf out of my sister's book and start reconnecting with the things that bring you joy. As we know, joy is one of the top ten positive emotions and has been shown to lift wellbeing and diminish depression. Combining the experience of joy with mindful activity can super-charge your recovery.

Ask yourself: What do I have in my life that I can engage in mindfully and that brings me joy?

By mindfully engaging in these special things in your life, you'll reap amazing benefits such as:

- reduced stress
- enhanced ability to deal with illness
- facilitation of recovery
- decreased depressive symptoms
- improved general health.[32]

Importantly, depending on the severity of your experience, mindfulness may not be enough to help you process and recover. Please speak to your GP and engage a qualified and experienced psychologist if you need professional intervention.

3 Re-evaluation

Once you start to feel more grounded, it's time to take a fresh look at the situation. With self-compassion at the forefront, consider your next move with these things in mind:

- What personal lessons can I extract from the experience?
- How can I move forward in a psychologically safe manner?
- What do I need to do to set myself up for resilience and sustainable growth in my next chapter?
- Who do I need on my side to achieve this?
- In future, what will I do if I notice early signs of this happening again?

And then:

- From an *emotional* perspective, what do I need in this next chapter of my life?
- From a *logical* perspective, what do I need in this next chapter of my life?

When you feel that you have arrived at a level of stability and your foundation has begun to rebuild, return to the C Word Method and start again.

4 Master fear

Examine the fears that came up for you during the experience. It's really important to be honest with yourself about these (and it may be a little confronting). Remember in Chapter 2, we talked about some of the common fears we experience, such as fear of:

- being less than perfect
- social or intimate rejection
- abandonment   lonliness
- humiliation
- vulnerability
- success.

Did any of these, or other fears, feature in your experience? Try to examine them dispassionately, as though you are watching yourself from above. Don't hook into the emotion of the fear, simply name it and own it.

Can you recall the self-talk that featured in your experience? What were you telling yourself about the situation that drove the fear? Now, looking back, how helpful and/or accurate was that self-talk?

Moving forward, what things can you tell yourself when these fears rear their ugly head?

SMART COURAGE

Remember the equation from Chapter 4? It's a key part of recovering and resetting after a crisis.

Smart Courage = emotional bravery + intellectual savviness

As we've already talked about, emotional bravery is about considering the full emotional impact of a decision, while intellectual savviness is about thinking a decision through in a thorough fashion.

So, as you reset and plan your move out of fear and into courage, it's time to take a new look at what is going to be the best for you emotionally and intellectually. It's important to keep in mind that what worked for you before may not work for you now – this is a new beginning and will require a renewed and thorough consideration about what is best for you.

Journal time

RESETTING WITH THE VAPOR MODEL

This might be a good time to 'get the vapors'. #thanksnanna

The VAPOR Model is a great way to evaluate how your confidence played out during the experience or crisis and, more importantly, what you can do differently next time.

Set aside some time – ideally quiet time where you won't be interrupted – to reflect on the following questions. Write your responses and reflections in your journal.

1. **Vulnerability** – How would you describe your vulnerability before the situation? What about during? Perhaps you showed too much or too little? Maybe you didn't connect with your vulnerability at all?

   Moving forward: How do you want your vulnerability to feature in your next chapter? Be really specific. How can you ensure that your vulnerability shows up as a strength?

2. **Assertiveness** – Looking back, were you being genuinely assertive prior to and during the experience? Or did you fall into the trap of being more aggressive or perhaps more passive?

   Moving forward: How can you ensure that your communication remains in the assertive zone?

3. **Positive emotion** – Which positive emotions featured in your world prior to the experience? What about during? How would you describe the role of positive emotions for you during this time?

   Moving forward: How can you intentionally introduce positive emotions into the next chapter? Specifically, which emotions will you focus on? Why?

4. **Optimism** – How would you characterise your optimism levels before and during the experience? High, medium or low? What role, if any, did optimism play in the experience?

   Moving forward: Step into the next chapter with the best-case scenario clearly in your focus.

5. **Resilience** – How would you describe your resilience levels prior to the experience? Would you say you were psychologically equipped to deal with and bounce back from this situation?

   Moving forward: What strategies can you put in place to ensure that next time something unexpected happens, you'll be in a strong position to cope and recover?

DEEP CONFIDENCE

I bet you are looking at people differently now . . . assessing their behaviour and wondering, are they overconfident or underconfident? Is their confidence authentic or is it being used to mask something else? Are they accessing their confidence from the inside or the outside?

And I wonder if you are starting to look differently at your beautiful self too? You've discovered some new tools to help you harness that Smart Courage and start stepping into Deep Confidence – the VAPOR Model is a great one to take with you especially for those times when life throws you a curve ball.

Oh, and if you're wondering how my sister Beck is going – well, as I write, she is moving through the VAPOR Model at her own pace. Something tells me she is about to embark on some big, empowered choices and changes in her life – and I for one can't wait to watch her blossom.

part
four

Fluid
Competence

FEAR
MASTERY

SMART
COURAGE

DEEP
CONFIDENCE

FLUID
COMPETENCE

> Some people want it to happen, some wish it
> would happen, others make it happen.
>
> MICHAEL JORDAN

The final part of this book is about making *it* happen – whatever *it* is for you. It's about holding accountability for your results, taking your destiny into your own hands and owning your outcomes.

This is where you'll see the C Word Method come to fruition; having mastered living alongside fear, stepped into Smart Courage and developed Deep Confidence, you're now ready to take all of these attributes and apply them to your life.

Fluid Competence is about drawing on your internal resources to springboard you into action – action congruent with your values and goals, action aligned with your life's purpose. When you're performing Fluid Competence you are in flow, connected to yourself and on purpose.

When I talk about 'performing' in life, I'm referring to operating at the level that is optimal for you – balancing your mental health with your desired results. I'm not here to drive you into burnout; I believe you have what it takes to invest in and nurture yourself, while also kicking some serious life goals.

FLUID
COMPETENCE

CHAPTER 10

YOUR

success

SWEET SPOT

I can never be safe; I always try and go against the grain.
As soon as I accomplish one thing, I just set a higher goal.
That's how I've gotten to where I am. The most alluring
thing a woman can have is confidence.

BEYONCÉ

AKA QUEEN B. JUJU. SASHA FIERCE

Sing it, Sista.

And she did – she sang and she danced and she promoted and she toured and she sang some more. She performed herself right into a burning pit of burnout.

Beyoncé has been honest about her experiences with burnout. She even stopped performing in 2011 so she could recover. As she said, 'It was beginning to get fuzzy – I couldn't even tell which day or which city I was at. I would sit there at ceremonies and they would give me an award and I was just thinking about the next performance. My mother was very persistent and she kept saying that I had to take care of my mental health.'[33]

What Queen B is referring to here is impaired cognitive functioning. The 'fuzziness' she talks about has been thoroughly examined by scientists and the link between work-related burnout and our capacity to think clearly is well documented. Recent research found that burnout is 'associated with cognitive impairment with the predominant deficits concerning executive functions, attention and memory'.[34]

So, for you, this means that allowing yourself to burn out can lead to issues with these thinking abilities:

- **Executive function** – Although it sounds like a fancy, boozy party in the top-floor boardroom, executive function actually refers to your capacity to coordinate and regulate your thoughts in order to move towards your goals. This is your brain's capability to actually process information and make sense of your world; it's your ability to make decisions and solve problems. Now, our friend Beyoncé may have had difficulty choosing between stilettos and trainers, or maybe it was more significant, like deciding which contract would benefit her career in a more sustainable way. When you reach burnout, this 'fuzziness' clouds your capacity to make smart decisions and it can become hard to trust yourself.

- **Attention** – Research shows that when you are burnt out your capacity to stay focused on a task becomes limited and you can be more impulsive. Your attention span can shrink and you may find it difficult to focus on more than one thing at a time. If I put myself in Beyoncé's fabulous shoes, I imagine a moment on stage would involve focusing on multiple things at once, from the beat of her music, to the movement of her dancers, to the spatial layout of the stage, to the lyrics she is singing, the steps she is dancing and the placement of several cameras. That's before she even considers the mood and reaction of her live audience as it changes moment to moment. Her cognitive load would be enormous. So when burnout is added to the mix, her brain becomes overloaded and unable to process these critical pieces of information, making her unable to do her job. While you may not perform on stage in a sequined leotard to millions of screaming fans, you probably do attend to loads of pieces of information in your daily life. If you reach burnout, your ability to do this is stunted and you might find yourself unable to effectively switch between different trains of thought (AKA your adaptive thinking).
- **Memory** – Can you imagine Queen B stopping mid-anthem on stage and saying to her audience, 'Oh, hang on, I forgot the rest of the song'? Or perhaps, sitting down in the middle of a dance break because she couldn't access the steps in her working memory? Or maybe going vague in an interview when being asked about her

223

favourite album? These things could have all been possible if she hadn't recognised her need to take time out. Some of the common early signs of burnout can be forgetting what you're saying mid-sentence, having difficulty finding a word that is 'on the tip of your tongue' or walking into a room to get something and forgetting what you were after. This is your short-term or working memory and it's critical in enabling you to function effectively in your work and life.

But burnout does not just impact your cognitive functioning. It is broader and more profound than you could imagine. The World Health Organization (WHO) defines burnout as a syndrome that results from 'chronic workplace stress that has not been successfully managed'.[35] According to WHO, burnout is an occupational phenomenon, occurring only in the workplace, and has three dimensions:

- feelings of energy depletion or exhaustion
- increased mental distance from one's job, or feelings of negativism or cynicism related to one's job
- a sense of ineffectiveness and lack of accomplishment.[36]

If you're feeling burnt out, you'll be:

- **exhausted** – you'll feel physically, mentally and emotionally drained
- **cynical** – you'll have a negative and pessimistic attitude
- **professionally ineffective** – you'll lose your cognitive, technical, practical, social and behavioural skills to do your job.

WE NEED TO TALK ABOUT JEMMA

Imagine you are in the office on a normal-as-any day. Your workmate Jemma is usually your partner in crime; you've always shared jokes, debriefed reality TV and whined about the boss together. But lately, you've noticed a few changes in Jem and are starting to worry about her.

For instance:

- She is usually full of energy and you would often go for a run or take a cardio class together at lunchtime. Now all she wants to do is sit at her desk and scroll through her phone. While Jem would usually be up for long and involved deconstructions of last night's TV or the latest political scandal, her recent responses are single-worded and abrupt. Where you would typically describe her as a go-getter, she currently seems really flat and can't find the energy to say or do anything outside of her job description.

- While you would always have a little whinge at work together and a joke at the boss's expense, Jem now seems to be stuck in negative mode. She doesn't seem to bounce back to her usually happy self, and always seems to find the dark side in any conversation. When talking about upcoming changes at work, she can only see the worst-case scenario and seems to be oblivious to the up-side of any argument. Where you would typically describe Jemma as a positive, happy force in the office, she's now more of a downer.

- In addition to her energy and attitude, you have become particularly worried about Jemma's work performance. She's supposed to be the 'smart one' in your team but lately she has been missing the mark. She has been forgetting basic things and missing small but important details, and she seems to be finding it difficult to make everyday work decisions. She has turned in a couple of pieces of work that have needed correction and the boss is starting to doubt her ability to complete her work accurately and on time.

As you reflect back over your observations of Jemma during the past 12 months, there were certainly some incremental changes. She gradually changed from believing she should 'do a good job', to driving herself to 'be the best of the best at all costs'. She was no longer satisfied with achieving solid results; she had to beat everyone else and was prepared to stay back as late as required to get ahead. Jem stopped engaging in her favourite activities like going to yoga, meeting friends for drinks and taking long lunches, instead focusing solely on getting ahead at work. She seemed to work harder and longer than everyone else and this started to become her 'new normal'.

So, what do you think? Is Jemma burnt-out?

Quite possibly.

THE SPACE BETWEEN HIGH PERFORMANCE AND MEDIOCRITY

Many business books preach the power of 'high performance' and often cite stereotypically male styles of working as the recipe for success: long hours, competitiveness, 'balls-out' risk-taking and brutal tactics to get ahead in the dog-eat-dog world.

Well, not only is this model of success biased towards a male thinking and working model, but it's completely outdated.

If you've ever watched the TV series *Mad Men*, you'll know what I mean about the mid-century, patriarchal version of work and success. It's no longer relevant nor effective (and it's certainly no longer okay to smoke and drink during business hours, while pinching your secretary on the bum!).

The term *high performance* drums up visions of sacrifice, taking risks at all costs and winning at the expense of others. It also sits very neatly on the pathway to burnout. So let's look at performance standards from a different perspective.

What would it mean to perform to your OPTIMAL levels?

The idea of optimal performance is more holistic and sustainable.

As I touched on in Chapter 5, professional athletes know that it's not ideal or even possible to perform at peak levels every day. They reserve their peak performance levels for specific timeframes to ensure their body and mind are ready to get results on game day. They aim to perform to their *optimal* level throughout the day-to-day training routine and this performance level is dynamic. Smart athletes know how to adjust their performance levels in the right way to ensure they expend more energy when required and preserve energy when it matters.

So *optimal performance* is when you intentionally moderate your physical, emotional and mental energy to ensure positive performance levels, relative to a particular situation. You achieve optimal performance levels when you have the self-awareness to monitor your performance and the flexibility to adapt your approach to match your needs and the needs of the task at hand. Performance at this level allows for ongoing learning and offers scope for life balance and satisfaction.

To apply this approach in your life, the key words are:

- **Moderation** – Tap into your self-awareness so you can keep tabs on yourself. This is about monitoring your energy levels but also your motivation and enjoyment of the task. The skill here is to know when you are pushing yourself too hard, or not hard enough, and to give yourself honest feedback about what needs to change.

- **Situation** – Optimal performance is dynamic and should change as the situation requires. Some tasks or projects require higher levels of exertion and focus than others, so it's important that you can change your approach to suit the situation, rather than applying the same levels of energy for every task.

- **Flexibility** – Your capacity to flex and adapt are critical to performing to your optimal levels. Getting stuck in 'one mode' leads to underperformance or overperformance, because one level will never be perfect for every situation. One size does not fit all when it comes to your performance.

- **Balance** – Gone are the days of glorifying workaholism. Today's positive performers are people who recognise the need for balance and breaks, for downtime and opportunities to recharge. We know that people who invest in self-care and have a holistic approach to self-management are more likely to achieve and maintain optimal performance.

**Optimal performance levels are the key to living
the experience of Fluid Competence.**

As we discussed with confidence, performance is something that is not necessarily 'the more, the better'. While underperformance leads to lack of results, overperformance might lead to temporarily strong results but these are likely to be unsustainable and may ultimately lead to burnout. Consider performance as sitting on a continuum (just like confidence does). I believe ideally you should sit somewhere between 6 and 8 out of 10 in order to achieve fantastic results, while also keeping things in perspective and looking after yourself.

UNDERPERFORMANCE					OPTIMAL PERFORMANCE			OVERPERFORMANCE	
1	2	3	4	5	6	7	8	9	10

Journal time

MY PERFORMANCE LEVELS

Consider your current approach to achieving results in your life. If you're really honest with yourself, where would you plot yourself today?

UNDERPERFORMANCE								OVERPERFORMANCE	
1	2	3	4	5	6	7	8	9	10

In your journal, answer these questions:

- What does this tell you about yourself?
- What insight does this offer about the results you have been achieving?
- If it's too high, do you believe you are at risk of burnout?

- If it's too low, have you considered *why* you are investing low levels of energy into this?
- What do you believe needs to change for you to operate at your optimal level?
- If you are currently between six and eight, what benefits do you notice? How does this level of energy facilitate your results, enable you to monitor your mental health and stay reasonably balanced in life?
- Are you currently achieving Fluid Competence?

In her 2021 book *The New Hustle: Don't Work Harder, Just Work Better*, Emma Isaacs, CEO of Business Chicks, proclaims that the hustle is dead and it's time for a new way of work. Emma's revised approach to work is all about being intentional and creative to get things done. It's less about how many hours you put in, and more about the quality of the results you achieve. It's the focus on optimal performance, which is sustainable, rather than pushing yourself so hard you burn out.

SETTLING, WITHOUT SETTLING

What if I told you, you don't need to give 100 per cent?

Would this sound like a strange thing to say, coming from me, a person who prides herself on courage, confidence and achieving amazing results?

I agree, it might sound a bit strange at first, but stay with me here . . .

Imagine you are about to purchase a new hairdryer. You want your hair dryer to have variable power levels, heat options, a variety of attachments such as a diffuser, a narrow piece and a comb nozzle. You have a price range in mind and you want it in the next week. With this criteria in mind, there would be hundreds, if not thousands of models on the market and a vast amount of information available for you to consume – YouTube videos, Google reviews, Facebook groups, hair stylist blogs, even influencer recommendations. You could invest several hours a day for the next week delving into everything there is to learn about all the hairdryer models that fit your criteria . . .

OR

. . . you could buy the dryer that satisfies your criteria, even if it's not the best possible choice. This is a decision-making process called **satisficing** where you choose an option that is satisfactory rather than optimal. A 'perfect decision' would require a great deal of effort to gather and review all the necessary information (and may not even be possible), whereas satisficing represents the kind of decisions you can make that meet your needs and don't require an excessive investment of time or energy.

In essence, satisficing is all about 'making "good enough" decisions instead of perfect ones'.[37]

I love this concept and I believe you can apply it across many areas of life, in addition to your decision-making. When it comes to performing to your optimal levels, you must monitor and manage your energy levels – you cannot afford to become bogged down in unnecessary details (especially if they will ultimately have little bearing on your overall result). This is less about taking short-cuts and more about becoming super discerning about where your highly valuable energy goes.

You could say, satisficing is the antidote to perfectionism.

I use an 80 per cent rule in my life. I focus on the 80 per cent that's important – these are my non-negotiables – and let go of the 20 per cent of details that aren't as important. Because I have strong belief in my capability, believe I can achieve what I set out to and have established 'good will' in many areas of my life, I feel the 20 per cent is worth the risk. The type of not insignificant but 'Okay by me' imperfections that might fall into this 20 per cent include:

- small spelling or grammar errors in a social media post
- tripping over my words in a live broadcast
- letting my shapewear slip out to be revealed on camera (yes, this actually happened!)
- calling someone the wrong name
- giving my daughter ice-cream for dinner after a crazy-busy day
- forgetting to celebrate Father's Day with my hubby
- leaving it too long between waxing appointments.

In the Grand Scheme Of Life, these things don't really matter. Because I have demonstrated to the world (that is, my family and friends, my social circles, my professional circles, my TV audience, my social media followers) that I am a good person with sound morals and values, no one is going to judge me too harshly. And if they do?

BLOCK >> DELETE >> NEXT

The secret to successful satisficing is self-compassion. When you come from a default place of self-acceptance and self-respect, your mindset is already programmed to be non-judgmental. This sets you up for an open and curious approach to problem-solving, giving yourself the benefit of the doubt and, importantly, trusting yourself that even if things don't work out, you'll be okay.

I could have died of embarrassment and beaten myself up when I saw my Spanx featuring on my thigh on primetime TV, but I didn't. (Well, not for long anyway.)

The key here is to recognise that the 20 per cent won't be perfect, but the 80 per cent will make up for it. I knew that my performance across an entire TV series gave me the credibility and reputation I needed to be 'forgiven' for a little thigh-support exposé.

To me, my TV performance looks like this:

80 PER CENT – IMPORTANT THINGS TO FOCUS ON AKA non-negotiables	20 PER CENT – LESS IMPORTANT THINGS TO FOCUS ON AKA negotiables
• Being authentic and true to my personal brand • Accuracy and appropriateness of my comments • Managing my energy and presence • Overall grooming, style and image • TV craft such as managing cameras and eye lines, listening to the producer in my earpiece, timing, clarity of communication, blocking (that is, where I'm placed in the space)	• Mis-speaking, stuttering or stumbling over my words • Wearing an outfit that is not 100 per cent flattering • Flat-hair moments • An unfavourable edit (within reason)

Journal time

SATISFICING

Consider the areas of your life where satisficing could help you to let go of some of the details that don't matter, and enhance your focus on the 80 per cent that counts.

Either in your journal or on this page, list examples of the type of things that would fall into the 80 per cent (important) and 20 per cent (less important) camps in each life area.

Career	Health
80%	80%
20%	20%

Family	Finance
80%	80%
20%	20%

Intimate relationship	Hobbies
80%	80%
20%	20%

Friendships	Travel
80%	80%
20%	20%

Take some time to think and write about whether your list above reflects your reality. Are your non-negotiables getting the priority they deserve?

Satisficing is a brilliant tool to have in your kit when it comes to avoiding burnout and ensuring a longer-term, more sustainable mode of operating. When you choose to operate at a 6 to 8 out of 10 in terms of your performance levels, you are telling yourself:

> I'm going to approach this task at an *optimal* level of energy, focus and attention. As long as I tick 80 per cent of the boxes, I'm satisfied that I'll achieve my goal and still have enough fuel left in my tank for my family/friends/health . . . and if the 20 per cent trips me up, I'll be okay.

Can you see the difference here? It's quite clear that this approach to life is something you can maintain in an ongoing way – it's not a sprint, it's a sustainable marathon.

THE IDEA

of optimal
performance

is more holisti

and

SUSTAINABLE.

WHAT IS FLUID COMPETENCE?

Imagine spending your life working towards a single and specific goal, achieving that goal, then quitting. What would it say about you, if you poured your life and soul into this one thing, then, once achieved, you simply turned your back and walked away?

This is exactly what Ash Barty, the 25-year-old Australian world number one women's tennis player, announced in early 2022. Ash, a three-time Grand Slam singles champion and the reigning champion at the Australian Open, made the shock decision to retire from professional tennis via an Instagram post. From the outside looking in, it seemed like a strange move – why would someone pull the plug on their career at the exact point that they reach the pinnacle?

Ash explained, 'It's exciting because there are so many things Ash Barty the person wants to achieve and dreams that I want to chase after. But I think my purpose won't change, I just get to contribute in a different way. I get to contribute more on the tennis side with the younger girls, younger boys, and throughout the communities, which is exciting for me.'[38]

Ash's purpose has always been clear – as a young Indigenous woman she has a strong drive to give back and support up-and-coming young people in sport. She has become an incredible role model, showing dignity and humility in her victories and making the courageous call to exit at the peak of her career.

No doubt, Ash's clarity of purpose made the decision much easier for her.

When it comes to Ash's core strengths, sure, her tennis acumen is at the top. But the breadth of her sporting prowess runs far beyond just tennis, as shown by her finishing first in the Brookwater Golf and Country Club ladies event just weeks after her tennis retirement. Yep, she won a golf tournament!

Ash may have retired from professional tennis, but she continues to **live on purpose** and **play to her strengths**. *These are* the key factors that differentiate functional competence from fluid competence.

Fluid Competence = purpose + strength

Clarity of purpose is about knowing what you want and WHY you want it. Optimal performers often tap into a higher purpose, something bigger than themselves to provide a values-driven, intrinsic motivation for the achievement of their goals.

Playing to your strengths is knowing and using your key strengths. Do you know your key strengths? Do you use them every day? Psychologists have found a clear link between using your strengths and achieving a state of 'flow', which facilitates improved performance.

I have to say, nothing builds your confidence like having clarity about what you're doing and why, and getting to live your strengths every day (more on strengths in the next chapter).

ANOTHER WORD ON JEMMA

Let's revisit our old mate Jemma, the poor burnt-out babe. When we left her earlier in this chapter she was a shell of her former self, having pushed herself beyond her limits. She had set her sights on an unrealistic goal and seemed to lose herself in the process.

How can we help Jemma to get out of this funk and start to rebuild her confidence?

First, it looks like she needs a 'wake-up call' to jolt her out of her current, unhealthy state. Perhaps some harsh feedback from her boss about her poor work performance, a health complication or a fractured friendship.

A wake-up call acts as a catalyst to help us change, but why is it that we often need something dramatic to happen to jolt us out of unhealthy states? Why do we let ourselves get to crisis point before we step in and take accountability for ourselves? I believe this tends to happen when we lose or lack self-awareness and are not disciplined about checking in with ourselves. When we let ourselves run on autopilot without asking 'Am I okay?' or 'Am I operating in a way that serves me?', we can travel in blissful ignorance – until something big happens to teach us a lesson. Your lesson here? Be self-aware, use your journal, monitor and review your own behaviour and consider whether your actions today are moving you towards or away from your goals.

Back to Jemma.

Once she finds self-awareness, whether through an external event or internal realisation, she's ready for our help. Let's imagine Jem joins you and me for coffee and a chat. How might we help her?

First, you explore her purpose, the bigger picture for her motivation and goals. Through clever, yet gentle questioning, you uncover her *real* purpose. Jemma responds:

> Yes, I was obsessed with getting a promotion. Once I made my mind up that this was what I wanted, I got tunnel vision. I couldn't focus on anything but my work, everything else just became unimportant. I know I let people down, including myself – I stopped caring about my health and fitness, my friendships, I even stopped dating.

You probe further: '*Why* was the promotion so important to you?'

Jemma reveals, 'It wasn't about blind ambition. It's my mum. She's really sick. We're really struggling financially and her treatment is costing a fortune. I figured if I could get the promotion and earn more cash, I'd be able to support her.'

(You've uncovered her clear purpose.)

Later on during the same coffee chat, you ask her, 'Do you enjoy working in this way?'

Jemma's eyes well up with tears. 'NO! I hate it. I feel absolutely exhausted but I don't know what else to do. I never enjoyed my job in the first place and now that it has become my whole world it just feels so wrong. I'm working with numbers all day but all I want to do is help people. I feel happiest and most connected when I'm using my nurturing skills, supporting others and showing empathy – not drowning in spreadsheets!'

(You have just uncovered one of her core strengths.)

Well done – you've managed to tap into Jemma's higher purpose and greatest strength.

Over the following weeks, you help Jemma to turn her life around. She reveals her mum's situation to her boss and asks to temporarily change her job structure – they agree to a compressed working week, across four days, and Jemma is permitted to work from home two days per week . This enables her to support her mum while still getting her job done and earning the same amount of money. You also help Jemma to realise that she is not suited to accounting and through your discussion, she discovers that she would really like a career in HR. Jemma decides to start studying HR when her mum is better.

If Jemma rated her confidence levels when she was working herself to the bone, it would have been three to four at most. Now, she has started living her purpose and is taking steps to play to her strengths, she would probably rate her confidence levels six to seven. Jemma is ready to step out of burnout and into the healthier and more productive state of Fluid Competence. This is her sweet spot.

Have you thought about your sweet spot when it comes to your performance in your career, relationships and life? Can you see yourself adjusting your approach to manage your energy levels, show self-compassion and focus on the critical 80 per cent? This is what I want for you and I suspect that you can already see that this is what you deserve.

Have you
thought about
your sweet spot
when it comes to
your performance
that you have
IN YOUR CAREER,
RELATIONSHIPS
and life?

UNKNOWN

FLUID
COMPETENCE

CHAPTER 11

I SHOULD
BE SO

lucky!

As you learned in the introduction to this book, I've endured some pretty gruelling online trolling over the years. I've been called a toxic feminist, a man-hater, a slut, a bitch and an imbecile and received a range of threats from 'You should be fired' (and the accompanying petition signed by 70,000 people to the same tune) through to 'If I see you, I'll rape you, then I'll . . .' You get the picture, I don't need to finish that one.

I've even been told to kill myself.

But time and experience have enabled me to turn the fear and anger into wisdom. These people and this type of behaviour do not intimidate me anymore; in fact, they barely register on my radar. I've become highly skilled at detaching from online hate and taking immediate action. BLOCK. DELETE. And if required, involve the police.

However, there is a different type of reaction that I still get from people that I cannot abide.

'You're SO lucky!'

No. I'm not lucky. I have worked bloody hard for decades to get to where I am today. I have taken risks, put myself in uncomfortable situations, faced rejection and humiliation, sought out education and mentoring, taken more risks, worked a bit harder and made loads of sacrifices.

Some of the more annoying statements I've endured have been:

- 'You're so lucky, you get to live in Bali!' No, I worked hard for years to enable me to have a flexible career. I sacrificed security and stability, and took the risk to move to a developing country with my partner and two-year-old daughter.
- 'You're so lucky, you get to have your nails, hair and make-up professionally done as part of your job!' Nope, not lucky. These little luxuries have come along as a fringe benefit of building a career that aligned with my values and personal beliefs.
- 'You're so lucky, you get to travel for work.' Sometimes, this means leaving my hubby and little girl for weeks or even months on end.

It gets lonely, I feel isolated and I desperately miss the support of my loved ones. It's not luck.

- 'You're so lucky, you have a great partner and beautiful, loyal friends.' Not luck, I get back what I put in. By showing kindness, empathy, compassion and love – most of the time (I'm not perfect) – I have attracted people with similar traits.

And of course, my favourite:

- 'You're so lucky, you're just naturally confident.' Sure, I may have been gifted with a genetic predisposition and socio-economic background for confident traits, but I take daily action to build and maintain my confidence. It doesn't just happen.

Can you relate? Have you ever been told you're 'lucky' when you know deep down that you have achieved success in your life due to your own strong will, resilience, sacrifices and hard work?

It's so frustrating.

Yes, I can appreciate that, from the outside, it may appear that we are lucky. As confident, competent, optimal-achieving women, we may make life look easy.

But how does it feel when someone (usually another woman) says to you, 'Everything comes so easily to you'? Don't you feel like screaming, 'I created this . . . it wasn't handed to me on a silver platter!'

One of the things we know about people who experience Imposter Syndrome is that they often attribute their own positive results to *external factors* ('It wasn't just me, the whole team contributed') and negative results to *internal factors* ('It's all my fault, I'm useless').

When someone tells you that they think you are 'lucky' to have achieved positive results, they are essentially IMPOSTERING you!

They are making the assumption that some mystical, magical force swept in and 'gave' you these results, rather than allowing for the possibility that you got off your butt and did it yourself! When another woman uses this style of communication, it is often delivered with a tone of jealousy – 'It's not fair, you're so lucky.' It is often a projection of her own feelings of inadequacy and her frustration that you are 'showing her up' by achieving positive results. It's a lot more about her than you.

Appearing 'lucky' is no coincidence. In fact, people who demonstrate the outward display of success are often performing Fluid Competence and they all have something in common.

Richard Wiseman, psychologist and professor at the University of Hertfordshire in England, has dedicated his life to understanding what luck is and how we can get more of it. In his book *The Luck Factor*, Wiseman reveals the approaches to life that turn certain people into luck magnets. His research has revealed that the key difference between *lucky* and *unlucky* people is the way they THINK.

According to Wiseman, so-called lucky people don't have magic powers, but they typically perform the following four daily habits.[39]

HABIT 1 – MAXIMISE YOUR CHANCE OPPORTUNITIES

Lucky people take action and action puts them where luck can find them. Unlucky people suffer analysis paralysis.

HABIT 2 – LISTEN TO YOUR INTUITION

Lucky people say their intuition guides them in their relationships, career choices and financial decisions. Unlucky people ignore it.

HABIT 3 – EXPECT GOOD FORTUNE

Lucky people are optimistic. In fact, 85 per cent of lucky people believe their dreams will come true. Will their dreams *actually* come true? It doesn't matter! It's this belief that drives them to take action in the direction of their goals, even in the face of hardship. Unlucky people only see obstacles.

HABIT 4 - TURN YOUR BAD LUCK INTO GOOD

Lucky people see the positive side of bad things that happen, and take action to prevent more bad luck. Unlucky people tend to focus on their own ill-fortune.

•

Based on these four habits, would you consider yourself lucky or unlucky?

Essentially Wiseman's research has revealed that perceived luckiness is achieved through the use of a range of mindset positions, thinking patterns and behavioural choices. You'll recognise these four habits, I'm sure, as I've touched on them throughout this book

In the C Word Method terminology, luck is achieved through:

- **A growth mindset** – believing things (and YOU) can change and everything is figure-out-able
- **Optimism** – focusing on the best-case scenario and using this belief as the basis for your decision-making
- **Taking action** – taking risks and experimenting with a range of options, extending your comfort zone
- **Cognitive balance** – listening to your intuitive, creative side and balancing this with logic and common sense (more on this in a moment)
- **Being kind** – achieving Wiseman's *contagious, upbeat energy* through showing positive regard, empathy, compassion and kindness for others (more on this in a moment too).

I'd like us to delve deeper into two of these: cognitive balance and being kind. I've selected these two because I believe they are critical skill-sets that can help you start to flourish in a way that serves you internally (by drawing on the full spectrum of your mindset and brain power) and externally (by fostering and building strong, positive relationships). This internal-external balance is another way to ensure you are moving from confidence to Fluid Competence.

BALANCED DECISION-MAKING

We talked earlier about the different thinking styles (AKA logical and emotional thinking) and the importance of using both. It seems apparent that people who strongly favour one type of thinking, without balancing it with the other, tend to make poorer decisions and could miss out on fantastic opportunities in life.

Well, it's time to talk about HOW. If you've been thinking in one dominant fashion for your entire life and it's completely ingrained in the way you live, how can you suddenly change this? Short of a brain transplant, how can you ensure that you approach important decisions (or any decision, really) in a smart and balanced way.

Enter, Walt Disney.

I bet you weren't expecting me to say that, were you?

Stay with me. The Walt Disney Method – also known as the Walt Disney Strategy or the Disney Method for short – is a creative thinking technique where you approach a project or a problem from three different perspectives: the dreamer, the realist and the critic. And then, once you've considered those three points of view, you can make the best, most competent decisions. Apparently, Walt Disney would use this three-perspective method whenever he was developing an idea for a film.

This technique is now used all over the world, from boardrooms to counselling sessions. It's not only a brilliant activity to use with couples and teams, but to use as your own personal decision-making tool too. I'm sure you can think of people in your world who are primarily a dreamer, a realist or a critic. But the real power of this activity comes into play when you realise that YOU have a dose of each inside you.

Sure, you might naturally gravitate towards one or enjoy using one more than the others, but when you can integrate all three, the power of your decision-making will exponentially grow.

By examining an issue from these three different perspectives, you'll ensure that you are not playing to a bias, that your choices are balanced and that you've anticipated potential objections. Fluid Competence is all about making the best possible decisions and choices in your life, because your decisions dictate the direction your life takes. So, accessing a technique such as this one will set you up for success.

Journal Time

THE WALT DISNEY METHOD

Consider a decision or choice you currently face in your life. Allocate three pages in your journal and write at the top of each, respectively:

- The Dreamer
- The Realist
- The Critic

Now, do some brainstorming or free association or stream of consciousness writing (basically, just write without editing yourself!).

On the Dreamer page, *only* write about the possibilities. What dream-like ideas could be pursued? What do you wish for?

On the Realist page, *only* write about the pragmatic steps and tactical things that would need to be put in place. What steps should be taken? What needs to be done?

On the Critic page, challenge the approaches of the Dreamer and the Realist. What could go wrong? Where are the risks and gaps? What points need to be considered and addressed before this decision can move forward?

Once your three pages are full, read through your notes and use a highlighter to identify the most important points. Start a new page in your journal and create the picture of your new broad perspective, your balanced and well-considered approach to this decision.

How will this impact your final decision?

#BEKIND

I'm sure you're aware of the #BeKind movement and social media trend of shining the spotlight on compassionate behaviour as a response to bullying and online abuse. I'm a huge advocate of being kind, as well as openly sharing and talking about kindness – you've probably even seen me online, proudly wearing my Be Kind T-shirt and sharing my thoughts about how we can benefit from being kinder to ourselves and each other.

But behind the slogans and influencer-led sponcon (social media speak for sponsored content) lies a powerful, evidence-based message. Being kind to yourself and to others can not only boost your confidence but also improve your overall quality of life.

The research shows that engaging in kind thoughts and behaviour can:

- strengthen your heart, through the production of oxytocin, which contributes to heart health and lowers blood pressure
- make you happier, because people who show kindness and generosity by donating to charity have been found to be happier in life
- keep you calm, through the production of serotonin which makes you feel more peaceful and also reduces depression and anxiety
- help you live longer, because people who volunteer to help others have increased longevity
- reduce your stress, because engaging in kindness decreases your cortisol (stress hormone) levels.[40]

So, how can you give yourself an uplifting kindness injection in your everyday life?

Here are two simple techniques that you can employ to engage the 'kind brain' and get those helpful hormones flowing:

1. **Get on the ARK** – This has nothing to do with Noah and his animal friends. It stands for Acts of Random Kindness. Pay for the coffee of the person in line behind you; pass on a parking space

that has some time left on the meter; smile at someone in the street who looks a little down; leave a glowing online review when you receive great service; pay someone a genuine compliment; or make an anonymous donation to charity. When you engage in these types of behaviour, without expecting anything in return, you gain the benefit of increased oxytocin and serotonin and decreased cortisol. This leads to more calm, happy feelings and less stress.

2. **Write a gratitude letter** – It sounds simple, but the act of writing a letter of thanks to someone who has had a positive impact on your life has been shown to have powerful and lasting benefits. Writing gratitude letters improves your wellbeing and reduces symptoms of depression.[41]

It's clear that engaging in smart, balanced decision-making as well as kindness can enhance your capacity to be 'lucky' or, as we now know it, 'confident and successful'.

YOUR MENSTRUAL CYCLE CAN MAKE YOU MORE CONFIDENT

This section relates to the menstrual cycle and its impact on hormone levels and, in turn, life. I understand that not all people who identify as women have periods, some women suffer medical conditions such as PCOS or endometriosis that may impact their periods and some women may be in perimenopause or menopause. If this section is not relevant for you, feel free to jump ahead.

•

I can't think of a better way to play to your smart decision-making while practising self-compassion than by listening to your body and your natural hormone cycle. Learning to sync your monthly cycle with your work and life schedule is the ultimate body-hack that can help you harness your energy and productivity.

Spoiler alert: You are MOST CONFIDENT when you are ovulating.

By learning the rhythms of your natural cycle, you can use your hormonal phases to guide you in timing major decisions, projects and goals in your life. During each phase of your cycle, you will have different strengths, so the key is to know what those are and when they are happening. Alisa Vitti, a menstrual health expert, author of the bestselling *WomanCode* and creator of the MyFlo app, says:

> If women are seeking to shift the imbalances created by the patriarchy, we must stop modelling our lives on a masculine biochemical 24-hour schedule. It's time to work based on a female paradigm of productivity, success and fulfilment.[42]

This just makes so much sense. If you're anything like me, you've probably got countless examples of times when you made bad decisions or got in your own way and then later thought, 'I was *so hormonal* when I made that decision.'

Let's take a closer look at what our own laywoman term 'so hormonal' actually means during each phase of our cycle, and how we can maximise our strengths during each phase. It's important to note, though, that everyone's cycle can be different and these phases can cross over with each other.

Starting with the first day of your period, you can map out your hormonal phases and make some smart choices about what to focus your energy on and when. The first phase is known as the **Creative Superstar** and can last between ten and 22 days.[43] During this time, you'll feel more creative, inspired and positive due to the increase in oestrogen. Start new projects, brainstorm and collaborate, plan out your creative work for the month or get out the whiteboard and go crazy with your mind-mapping (using every coloured pen you can get your hands on!).

The one to three days that surround ovulation are known as your **Active Communicator** phase. Your hormone levels before, during and after ovulation support the function of the verbal and social centres of your brain, encouraging you to be more externally focused. This is a great time to initiate those tricky conversations with your boss or partner, to bring together like-minded people for collaboration and, of course, to schedule in catch-ups with your A-list friends.

Following ovulation, the next 14 days or so are considered your **Dark Horse** phase (sounds ominous, I know!). I'd prefer to call this your **Chill-Out** phase because the increase in progesterone produces a calming effect, encouraging you to slow down as your energy reduces.[44] You may become more inwardly focused during this time, so it's a good idea to schedule your quiet, detail-focused work, perhaps even solo projects. Also, as you may feel a little emotionally flat during some of this time (PMS may even show up) it's a good idea to proactively put some self-care strategies in place – book that massage, reach out to your supportive friends or schedule in some quiet time.

The final one to five days of your cycle, crossing over with phase 1, are considered your **Intuition and Recharge** phase.[45] This is when you may experience your period. In addition to dealing with any symptoms of your period, this is a good time for personal reflection. Your intuition may be heightened during this phase, so take the opportunity to listen to your (probably bloated) gut, reflect on the month that was and consider your hopes for the month to come. Being in a more reflective space can be really positive for contemplating goals, especially when it comes to evaluating your performance on past goals. Between cramps, try to extract the lessons from your last month and consider what you could do to enhance your happiness and success next month.

Why don't you try conducting an experiment with your next cycle? Use your cycle as a guide to map out what you choose to do and when. At a high level, plan your creative, strategic work for the first half of your cycle and your more detailed work for the second half. Got an important presentation, date or event? See if you can schedule it for around your ovulation phase for maximum confidence and grit!

Journal time

CYCLE SYNCING

Grab your diary and start mapping out your next cycle and life schedule.

First, break the month into two parts:

- Strong, Creative Superstar (Follicular Phase) – in the first two weeks of your cycle, starting from day one of your period, plan for activities that require creativity, energy, imagination and memory
- Dark Horse (Luteal Phase) – in the final two weeks of your cycle, after ovulation, plan for lower energy and more detailed tasks that require your focus and concentration

Next, estimate the date you'll be ovulating (around day 14) and try to schedule in any activity that requires **top notch social skills** and **confidence**.

Then, identify when your next period is likely to arrive and plan for some **self-reflection** and **self-care** during that time.

After syncing your cycle with your life schedule for two months, reflect in your journal on any particular changes you noticed over that time.

THE POWER OF ACCEPTANCE

In the early noughties, a girlfriend and I decided to take a trek through the north of Thailand, all the way up to the border of Myanmar. This is one of the most physically challenging things I've ever done – carrying a heavy backpack through rugged, thick jungle terrain, up painfully steep and slippery muddy hills, in 100 per cent humidity and around 40-degree heat. Climbing one of those hills, with a large stick in hand for balance, was one of the first times I can recall going into a trance state through my breathing. Focusing on one step in front of the other, trying not to slip and slide all the way to the bottom, I remember counting my breaths and listening to my pumping heart as I told myself, 'Keep going, nearly there.' It became meditative for me and enabled me to stay in the moment, be totally present and minimise my stress and anxiety (I would later draw on this same technique when experiencing a miscarriage and, again, found it to be incredibly helpful).

The trek lasted for several days and on one of the days the overnight rain had been so heavy that our path was completely blocked. To get to our next destination, we would have to go via the river. I remember sitting in awe as we watched our local guides build rafts out of tree branches and reflecting on how lucky we were going to be to have a chilled-out day of drifting on hand-crafted rafts ahead of us.

But the rafts weren't for us – they were for our backpacks.

We were advised to don a lifejacket and enter the river. The realisation soon dawned on us that we had five hours of river swimming ahead to get to our camp for the night. The journey started out as a relaxing cruise – our life jackets kept us buoyant as we comfortably drifted down the gently bubbling river. There was a group of us from all over the world and we used our cruising time to get to know each other, sing songs together and laugh our way through the soothing waters.

Then, it all changed.

We hit the rapids.

I have no idea how long the first period of rapids lasted, but it was brutal. My body was thrown against rocks and sharp edges and I had a sense of complete loss of control. The river pulled me under, spat me out and threw me around like a discarded bath-toy. My first instinct was to fight, so my body stiffened and I resisted every ebb and flow. I remember the sensation of the harsh water and rocks, feeling like knives one moment, heavy bricks the next. Then, just as quickly as it started, it stopped.

We suddenly returned to a calm, soothing phase of the river and a chance to recover. I examined my arms and legs, covered in throbbing cuts and bumps, and knew that I had done some damage. As a group, we started to debrief and soon realised that we were in a completely unpredictable situation with no control over our bodies. I remember being filled with dread and thinking, 'There is no way I can go through that again.' We couldn't get out and walk because the path was still flooded, so we had no choice but to keep going in the river. Before I knew it, I was enveloped in another rapid surge and, still feeling stressed and flooded with adrenaline, I stiffened up again and felt every rock my limbs thrashed against.

At some point during this five-hour experience I must have realised that fighting the rapids was only making life harder. I recall taking myself mentally back to the hill-climb meditation experience and telling myself to just ACCEPT it. When the next rapid surge came I didn't fight it – I remember feeling like a floppy rag doll and allowing the river to take me where she needed to take me. I didn't resist, I just focused on keeping my head above the water and the rest of my body became one with the water. I listened to my breathing, slowly counted and waited for the aggressive river to find calm again. And she did. This time, I noticed it didn't hurt as much, it wasn't as stressful, and I started to believe that I could get through the next few hours.

This cycle continued, entirely unpredictably, for several hours when, eventually, we made it to our campsite for the night.

Warm beer and cold noodles have never been so appealing!

I have to admit it took me many years to extract the core lesson from this experience. For a long time I reflected on the experience as a 'great story' and recounted the traumatic event at dinner parties, re-enacting each dramatic chapter.

But eventually I realised that this story was about the power of acceptance.

It seems so obvious now. As psychologist Carl Jung said, *What you resist, persists*. This lesson in acceptance was one that I really needed to learn – I wonder if this is similar for you? I naturally prefer to take matters into my own hands and uncompromisingly take action towards my goals (which, of course, is what the majority of this book is about). So for me, giving over control and accepting that things are beyond my influence has been a really hard lesson to learn.

You might say I had to be smashed against fierce water rapids and sharp rocks for five hours in order to get it!

The bigger lesson here is learning to identify when to *push and drive* yourself, versus *allowing* and going with the flow. I suggest that in situations where you have control, go for it, drive yourself towards the goals you desire. But when you find yourself in an experience that is partially or completely outside of your control, consider loosening your hold on the reins.

WHAT YOU

RESIST,

persists

You might be familiar with the Serenity Prayer practised in many 12-step recovery programs:

> God, grant me the serenity
> To accept the things I cannot change;
> Courage to change the things I can;
> and wisdom to know the difference.

Whether the spiritual aspect resonates with you or not, I'm sure you'll agree that the wisdom here is powerful.

Take this wisdom and the other approaches we have discussed in this chapter, from luck and kindness to being aware of your cycle, to think about the common situations in your life, your degree of control and your preferred approach. Here's an example, followed by a chance for you to have a turn in your journal:

SITUATION	LEVEL OF PERSONAL CONTROL	MY APPROACH
Seeking a promotion at work	High	Create my own luck; use a balanced decision-making style; show compassion for colleagues; play to my cycle and schedule interview for the second week of my cycle (as close to ovulation as possible)
Living in a locked-down situation due to global pandemic	Low	Practise acceptance; meditate; maintain a growth mindset and optimistic attitude; be kind to myself and others

Journal time

ACTION VS ACCEPTANCE

First, spend five minutes brainstorming all the important decisions or situations in your life that require your attention and focus.

Then, draw three columns in your journal with the headings: Situation, Level of Personal Control and My Approach. Follow my example on the previous page and map out your action or acceptance for each one.

This is likely to draw out some key personal insights for you. Take some time to reflect on your new insights in your journal:

- What did this activity tell you about your control over the challenging situations in your life?
- What have you discovered about 'acceptance' as a tool? Where do you see opportunities to use this more in your life?
- If you were to practise acceptance in ONE area of your life, what impact would this make? How would this change your self-talk? Your emotional state? Your decisions and choices?

FLUID
COMPETENCE

CHAPTER 12

GIVING HEAD TO

get ahead

(NOT A CHAPTER ABOUT PORN)

I thought long and hard about the title for this chapter. I absolutely hate this expression. I hate everything it says about women and ambition and competence, and it makes me angry.

So, I'm reclaiming it.

What we KNOW is that dolling out sexual favours for men is the last thing women need to do to get ahead in our careers, relationships and life. We already have most of the skills, knowledge and attributes we need to succeed in life; we just need a little nudge to remind us that we CAN do it and we DESERVE it.

For me, 'Giving Head To Get Ahead' now means
'Using Your Emotional Intelligence To Win At Life'.

In her game-changing book, *The Authority Gap: Why Women Are Still Taken Less Seriously Than Men, And What We Can Do About It*, British author and BBC journalist Mary Ann Sieghart conducted a broad review of the research and literature on the global gender gaps in authority, perception of competence and, ultimately, leadership. Her findings have the potential to change the conversation about women and success.

Sieghart examined the evidence on gender differences in intellectual ability and found that:

- From an early age, girls outperform boys. They develop faster, learn to talk earlier, develop self-discipline at an earlier age and use broader vocabulary.
- Girls get better grades at school than boys, particularly in humanities, but also in maths and science in some countries and outnumber boys at university.
- On average, girls and women are exactly as intelligent as boys and men.

There is no doubt that women's cognitive abilities are every bit as good as men's. So, what else could account for the massive chasm between our respective representation in the top jobs?

Sieghart dipped into gender differences in personality, and looked at the data on the Big 5 personality traits: extraversion, agreeableness, openness, conscientiousness and neuroticism. Her review of the global research found that the two personality traits that are most often correlated with leadership – extraversion and openness – are typically at the same level for women and men. But if we look into the deeper sub-scales:

- Women score higher on warmth, positive emotions, gregariousness and activity.
- Men score higher on assertiveness and excitement-seeking.

Makes sense, doesn't it? All our own anecdotal evidence tells us that, typically, women are better at utilising emotional intelligence and men are better at being competitive. Women are better at 'transformational leadership' and men are better at 'authoritative leadership'. These findings reinforce the message that:

Men might make better leaders if they were warmer and more positive, and women, if they were more assertive.

When it comes to building our assertiveness (which is really *confidence in action*) we have certainly made some inroads over the generations. According to Sieghart, compared with how women judged themselves on the same criteria decades ago, today's women self-report as more ambitious, more self-reliant and more assertive but they have not lost their traditionally feminine traits such as affectionateness or understanding.[46]

WHAT IS THE OPPOSITE OF ASSERTIVENESS?

Okay, that was a trick question.

Assertiveness actually has two opposites: aggression and passivity. The challenge for you, my friend, is to figure out which one is your default. But first, let's understand what assertiveness really is.

Have you ever noticed that when a woman stands up for herself, asks for her needs to be met and uses non-emotional language, she gets labelled a BITCH? Yet, when a man exhibits the same behaviour he is labelled a GO-GETTER or even a LEGEND? Me too. Obviously, there is a well-established patriarchal system at play here that needs women to feel and act in a submissive way in order to function. While we can't change the way the patriarchy is constructed (today), what we can change is the way we show up and use our voices.

Assertiveness is about asking for your needs to be met in a direct and dispassionate manner, while acknowledging the emotional tone of the room.

When you are being assertive, you are:
- grounded and centred in your space
- showing equal respect for yourself and others
- using sound evidence to back up your argument
- focused on problems and solutions, rather than people and emotions
- demonstrating empathy for others, without diminishing your own status
- seeking a win-win outcome (where possible)
- recognising the broader context in which you are operating, and adjusting your approach accordingly
- utilising non-verbal communication to demonstrate your power, without being overbearing
- smiling (because, warmth).

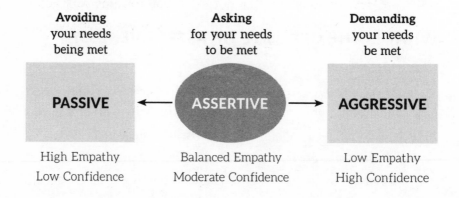

Avoiding your needs being met	Asking for your needs to be met	Demanding your needs be met
PASSIVE	← **ASSERTIVE** →	**AGGRESSIVE**
High Empathy	Balanced Empathy	Low Empathy
Low Confidence	Moderate Confidence	High Confidence

Consider the diagram on p. 262 and reflect on your own natural style. Over the 20 years I've been working with women, especially in the workplace, I've observed that most have a default non-assertive go-to position.

If they are not being assertive in a certain situation, they tend to gravitate to a **passive stance** where they:

- are highly 'other-focused'
- avoid asking for their needs to be met
- acquiesce to others rather than stating their opinion
- raise others to a higher level of status
- respect the needs of others before their own
- make themselves physically smaller
- feel regret over missed opportunities.

Or they gravitate to an **aggressive stance** where they:

- are highly 'self-focused'
- impose their needs and expectations on others
- dominate the conversation and speak over others
- don't listen
- show little empathy or compassion for others
- physically dominate others
- regret their behaviour after it occurs.

I'm here to tell you that both passive and aggressive communication styles are dysfunctional and will not move you towards your goals. Raising your own awareness about your non-assertive default style can be really helpful in learning to adapt.

MEN MIGHT MAKE BETTER

leaders if they

*were warmer
and more positive,*

and women, if
they were more
ASSERTIVE.

Journal time

WHEN I'M NOT BEING ASSERTIVE

Reflect on the last time you can remember being non-assertive. Hint: if you were being passive you may have later had regrets that you missed an opportunity and if you were being more aggressive, you may have later felt a little uncomfortable about stepping on someone's toes.

With this situation in mind, ask yourself:

- What triggered my non-assertive reaction?
- At what exact moment did I realise I was being passive/ aggressive?
- How did I feel when I was being passive/aggressive?
- On a scale of 1 to 10, how effective was my approach?
- How strong was my feeling of regret later, when I realised I had been too passive/aggressive?
- Next time I'm faced with a similar situation, what can I do differently in my thinking (self-talk), emotional response, choices and behaviour?

SPOTLIGHT ON JASMINE | FIND YOUR VOICE

As a widow and single mother with a successful career in fashion, Jasmine was proud of her accomplishments. She had overcome so much in terms of grief and loss, supporting her children through the loss of their dad, and had gone on to build an enviable career over the past five years.

At last, she believed she was ready for a new relationship. Obviously, the stakes were very high for her – she didn't want to introduce her kids to just anyone and she was hesitant about sacrificing her precious spare time for a man. With solo parenting, managing a demanding career, connecting with her wonderful friends, her dedication to her fitness and the occasional night out, she had very little time to herself. But Jasmine started to notice that she felt lonely and developed a real yearning to share her world with an equally busy and self-sufficient man.

Fast-forward 12 months and Jasmine had created a new relationship with a man called Freddy. They had so much in common: they went to the gym together and shared a passion for healthy food; they both enjoyed the active lifestyle and, at face value, appeared to have similar values about family. They were having a great time together and when she introduced Freddy to her kids, he was a hit! Jasmine's kids loved playing sports with Freddy and, as a group, they all had loads of fun together.

So when Freddy started using abrupt language with Jasmine, she barely noticed at first. On the whole, their relationship was great and it was heading towards a serious commitment, and she figured no one was perfect . . . surely a few harsh words didn't really matter?

He had briefly mentioned that his previous marriage had been very volatile, with lots of tension and yelling. Jasmine rationalised this by telling herself he must have married an unstable woman.

But over time Jasmine developed the impression that Freddy started to resent her career. Although he initially said that he loved her independence, he seemed to become less supportive and more critical of her career as the months passed. It wasn't just 'what' he was saying to her about her career, it was more about 'how' he spoke to her. Jasmine felt that he was belittling her, speaking down to her as though he thought he was superior to her, and, critically, he seemed threatening in his language. Although never physically overbearing, Freddy used his words to undermine her confidence and create self-doubt in her. He often referred to the 'selfishness' of her having a demanding career when she should be fully focused on her children. His tone was often highly judgmental, blaming her for any issues that arose with her kids. He also threatened to leave her on a regular basis, especially as an ultimatum if she wouldn't reduce her focus on her job. This often left her feeling deflated, powerless, incompetent as a mother and pretty hopeless.

Looking back, Jasmine's relationship with her late husband had been very warm and supportive. He rarely challenged her and when he did, it was gentle and non-judgmental. If anything, she was the dominant one in that relationship and she never really had to 'stand up for herself'. She had entered the new relationship with Freddy as a passive partner, as a woman without a strong voice in her relationship (which she found ironic, as she had no problems speaking up in the office).

Jasmine reached her tipping point when her boss offered her the opportunity to lead a high-profile project and Freddy point-blank refused to allow her to take it. It would involve longer hours and more travel, and he told her that neglecting her children like this would damage them permanently. And, true to form, he threatened to leave her if she took up the opportunity.

In the moment, Jasmine vaguely agreed with Freddy to keep the peace, but something shifted inside her.

Jasmine and I sat down together for one of our regular sessions. She unpacked the whole situation for me, through frustration and tears. She talked about her initial reaction to passively agree with Freddy and sacrifice her career advancement, and the accompanying inner conflict she experienced. Although her words said yes, her whole body was screaming NO!

We spent some time together exploring the practical aspects of her situation (such as the financial benefit for her family if she took the position, the need for additional child-care support and the logistics of travel) as well as the more emotional aspects (her sense of identity and accomplishment, her capacity to feel proud of herself and her confidence levels). But, most importantly, we uncovered Jasmine's deep, core motivation for wanting to take the role – she desperately wanted her children to see her as a positive role model.

It was this desire that empowered her to change her communication style with Freddy. By channelling this motivation, Jasmine found clarity and a level of courage she had never tested before. She really liked Freddy and wanted to continue the relationship but not if he stood in the way of her career or if he continued speaking to her in a disrespectful way.

Now, as you know, I'm all about expanding the comfort zone rather than jumping into the anxiety zone, so we agreed Jasmine would take baby steps. While she was clear on her message, she didn't feel comfortable yet to transition from passive communication to verbally assertive communication. So she wrote Freddy a letter. She covered everything she wanted from the relationship, her expectations about Freddy's communication with her (especially in front of her kids) and her need to balance both career and parenting responsibilities – and she even showed empathy for the impact on him. We both agreed it was a thoughtfully constructed letter, ticking off all the characteristics of assertiveness.

I'd love to report that Freddy read the letter and immediately changed his tune, but you know what they say about the leopard? He actually doubled-down on his position. This time, Jasmine was steadfast. She was clear on what she wanted, what she deserved and what her deal-breakers were. She chose to walk away from the relationship and invest the extra time in her career and family.

Although her relationship with Freddy didn't have the 'happy ending' Jasmine was hoping for, she learned an invaluable lesson. She discovered her own WHY (being a positive role model for her kids) and started to practise assertiveness. Not such an unhappy ending after all.

THE POSITIVE NO

I'd love to introduce you to one of my favourite assertiveness techniques.

It's called the Positive No and it's a brilliant tool to help you say NO when the situation is a bit tricky or the stakes are high. This was developed by William Ury, co-founder of the Harvard Program on Negotiation and one of the world's leading experts on negotiation and mediation. It's a three-step process that works like this:

YES >> NO >> YES

1. **Say YES to yourself.** First, you check in with your own values and goals and ask yourself what would best serve your own needs. This is essentially an 'internal yes'; you don't say it aloud, just to yourself.

2. **Say NO to the other.** Then, you offer a definitive NO that asserts your power and sets clear boundaries.

3. **Offer an Alternative YES.** Lastly, you offer an alternative suggestion that furthers your relationship by presenting a possibility that is consistent with your needs and values.[47]

So, let's put the *Positive No* into practice.

Let's say you are currently saving up for a deposit on your first property. This is something that means the world to you and you have been diligently putting away a percentage of every pay and being really careful with your discretionary spending. You have set a clear goal to have the money you need by the end of the year and you're on track. This gives you an incredible feeling of accomplishment and a sense of pride in yourself.

Your friend comes to you with an exciting invitation to a fancy corporate marquee at the races next weekend. It will be a day full of champagne, fancy food, fashion and men in lovely suits . . . and tickets are $400. It sounds like so much fun and you love the idea of getting out of your grubby tracksuit pants and into a fabulous frock for the day!

It's a tricky situation with competing pay-offs. You feel a little cognitive dissonance (the state of having inconsistent thoughts, beliefs or attitudes), so you decide to use the Positive No technique:

1. **You say YES to yourself.** Your top priority right now is your savings goal. If you were to invest $400 in a day at the races, plus the cost of a dress, fascinator, shoes, hair and make-up, manicure and pedicure, spray tan and dress thongs (yep, it's an Aussie thing), you'd end up around $1000 behind in your savings goal.

2. **You say NO to your friend.** Just no.

3. **You offer an alternative YES to your friend.** As another option, you might ask where the girls will be having post-races cocktails and suggest meeting up there at the end of the day. Or you might invite them around to your apartment for a pre-races champagne breakfast. Thus, you maintain the positive emotional bond with your friend, while standing in integrity and being true to yourself.

Give the Positive No technique a try next time you are faced with a tricky decision.

Assertiveness, while a critical skill in a confident woman's toolkit, is not the only way to communicate for success. Remember, the reclaimed title of this chapter is 'Using your emotional intelligence to win at life', so I think it's time to examine what emotional intelligence, or EQ, really is and how we can tap into this feminine superpower to get ahead.

EQ – THE REAL FEMALE SUPERPOWER

I truly believe the most powerful difference between women and men is our innate capacity for empathy, connection and the successful formation of deep relationships. For better or worse, women are wired to connect in a more urgent fashion and it underlies most of our angst and our awe.

I'll bet if you were to reflect back on the most significant emotional highs and lows in your life, they'd mostly be related to your human connections. As women, we tend to prioritise our emotional and relational experiences over the practicalities; we know that if things are balanced and positive in our relationships, we can take on the rest of life with aplomb.

For many of us, this can be a double-edged sword. While it gives us perceptiveness and strength in our relationships with partners, friends, family and colleagues, it can also be a burden when it comes to the more practical aspects of life. At times, we can trip over our empathy.

'Mel, you're tripping over your empathy again' was something an early mentor of mine would often chastise me with. Looking back, I think perhaps he meant to say something like, 'Mel, your emotional intelligence is still developing and you haven't found your balance yet. Keep going, you'll get there', but who am I to put words in his mouth?

Of course, emotional intelligence or EQ is more than simply the demonstration of empathy. Daniel Goleman is best known for his writing on emotional intelligence and is Co-Director of the Consortium for Research on Emotional Intelligence in Organizations at Rutgers University. His model of emotional intelligence helps us to see that there are four separate domains of EQ that we can develop. These competencies are all 'learnable' skills that you can build (which means they can also diminish if you don't use them for a while).

THE EMOTIONAL INTELLIGENCE OF THE C WORD METHOD

Goleman defines the four global domains of EQ as:

- self-awareness
- self-management
- social awareness
- relationship management.

I'm sure none of these terms are new to you (especially since you have made it to the final chapter of this book). You're probably highly aware that we have been speaking about all four of these concepts throughout *The C Word* – emotional intelligence is one of the underlying principles of my work. I'll show you how what you've learned through the C Word Method directly connects with your emotional intelligence.

Self-awareness

Self-awareness means being aware of your own emotions, and being able to identify them correctly. This is the most important of the EQ skills. It allows you to recognise your own strengths and weaknesses. If you are aware of your feelings, you know what causes you to feel happy, proud, alarmed, disgusted and so on. These are your biases – positive as well as negative.

All of the work you have been doing in your journal throughout the course of reading this book has been building self-awareness. Every time you pause to take an honest look at yourself, reflect, consider and examine your thoughts, feelings and behaviours, you are building your self-awareness. Self-awareness forms the foundation of all sustainable behavioural change. Throughout this book I have introduced you to self-awareness with lessons about:

- the signs of stress
- creative brain vs logical brain functions
- the relationship between anxiety and courage
- catastrophic thinking patterns
- common mistakes women make
- the little girl hangover
- ideal confidence levels
- self-esteem and self-efficacy
- optimism
- resilience.

As you become consciously aware of your own thinking patterns, moods, habitual reactions to certain situations and historical influences, your power base builds. You stop being a victim to automatic thinking and behavioural patterns and start to step into an empowered position where you can choose how you respond.

Self-awareness is one of the key success factors in relationships, career and life. You gain an immeasurable confidence boost when you can hook into your self-knowledge and boldly predict how you will show up in a given situation. Knowing yourself at this level also requires a good dose of acceptance, because you probably won't love everything you learn about yourself, so it's about balancing the things you celebrate with the things you accept.

Here's an example of self-awareness: 'I get nervous around authority figures, especially my boss, and this is because my father was a dominating figure who never listened to me.'

Self-management

Self-management is the ability to control your emotional reactions while still behaving with honesty and integrity. A woman who is emotionally intelligent does not let bad moods or a strong emotional reaction govern her behaviour. She is able to be honest and frank in a calm manner, without attacking others.

If self-awareness is about understanding yourself, self-management is what you *do* with that information. This is about the choices and decisions you make, based on your understanding of your own beliefs, values, strengths, needs and desires, in order to set yourself up for success. If your self-awareness tells you that you need lots of emotional validation in a relationship, yet you choose a partner who is emotionally stunted, this would be a demonstration of poor self-management. But if you used this self-knowledge to make a choice that is in your best interests – that is, selecting a partner who enthusiastically validates you – this would be considered a good self-management decision. Throughout this book I have introduced you to self-management with lessons about:

- reframing unhelpful thinking patterns
- changing the meaning of fear
- understanding Imposter Syndrome
- the difference between reacting and responding
- the benefits of metacognition (thinking about your thinking)
- understanding that the brain can change in response to new thinking patterns
- fixed versus growth mindset
- the difference between your comfort zone and the anxiety zone
- the benefits of confidence
- the VAPOR model
- the power of positive emotion
- rebuilding confidence after a crisis
- dealing with burnout

- optimal (rather than high) performance
- satisficing
- Fluid Competence
- the real meaning of luck
- the Disney Method.

When you start to use these types of techniques and incorporate a more conscious and mindful approach in life, you will begin to feel more in control, more confident. This is where you'll start to engage in little self-experiments, trying on different thinking styles and observing the results. You'll learn to trust yourself more and feel more stable in your relationships.

Here's an example of self-management: 'Because I know I get nervous around authority figures, I choose to plan my interactions with my boss and prepare notes and evidence to support my argument. Wherever possible, I bring up important issues with my boss in the presence of a trusted colleague so I can feel supported. I always make sure I give myself some time for recovery after these interactions so I can recharge my energy and continue to show up as my best self at work.'

Social awareness

Social awareness has two parts: empathy and attention. Empathy means being able to sense what the other person is feeling, and to know what their emotion feels like from your own experience. It does not necessarily mean you agree with the other person. Attention is about knowing how other people are reacting, or anticipating how they are likely to react, to what you do and say.

Social awareness is a bit like being politically aware in your social world. It's about 'reading the room', testing the social climate and informing yourself of the tone before you respond. Throughout *The C Word* I have introduced you to social awareness with lessons about:

- toxic femininity
- gender differences in the demonstration of courage
- confidence as a skill-set
- confidence from the outside in and inside out
- kindness
- the power of acceptance.

Social awareness gets you 'out of your own head' and enables you to see the world from the perspective of others. It's a critical skill in helping you to influence others as it enables you to tap into their needs. This skill-set helps you see beyond the practicalities of a situation and identify the emotional hooks that will help you work towards win-win outcomes.

Here's an example of social awareness: 'I understand that my boss has recently lost his mother and is dealing with some tough organisational politics at the moment. I imagine he is feeling a little sad and possibly vulnerable in the work environment. I would anticipate that this might make him more reactive than usual, so I'll tread lightly.'

Relationship management

Relationship management includes the ability to communicate in a clear and convincing way. Being clear means being able to say what you mean simply, and being able to offer examples. It relies on understanding how people feel and what emotions are important in their decision-making process. A person who is emotionally intelligent can communicate ideas, information and requests to others effectively. They pay attention to how others are reacting and adjust their approach to get a better result.

When someone is described broadly as a 'good communicator', they are probably skilled in relationship management. This skill-set is the culmination of self-awareness, self-management and social awareness applied together. It is the capacity to start from a place of clear self-understanding, making smart choices to bring out your own best characteristics, reading the room and making smart choices to build rapport and relationships for shared positive outcomes. Throughout this book I have introduced you to relationship management with lessons about:

- expanding your comfort zone
- the power of the first step
- assertiveness.

Managing relationships is a dynamic and ever-evolving process; you'll never stop learning. Every moment of every day, you receive information from the people in your life about how to treat them. Listen to them, watch them closely and observe when their words and behaviours don't match up. (My tip: trust the behaviour over the words every time.)

Here's an example of relationship management: 'I've learned that my boss appreciates data and bottom-line benefits, so I always lead with the numbers and follow up with the human impact. I know he responds well to praise so I offer positive feedback before I ask for something. My boss tends to be in a good mood (and more open to ideas) on Friday afternoons so I make the most of these windows when pitching ideas.'

●

Did you notice that the list of lessons we covered on self-management was much longer than the others? This was quite intentional. My hope for you is that this book will be a helpful, practical resource that you can revisit when needed, so it's very much focused on the skills you can apply in managing yourself – AKA self-leadership. Self-leadership is really another way to describe Fluid Competence. When you have moved through the C Word Method and therefore mastered living alongside fear, stepped into Smart Courage and developed Deep Confidence, you'll be prepared to lead yourself into Fluid Competence. Nothing says 'I'm the leader of my own life' like a woman who takes calculated risks in order to move towards her goals.

CONCLUSION

THE POWER OF ONE LITTLE WORD

I'm aware that many of the ideas and lessons in this book have taken a bit of brain power – some may have challenged you, some may have bored you, but many of them got you thinking. So I'd like to break it down and share one of the most powerful, yet simplest lessons I've ever learned about mindset, and it all comes down to one little word.

My daughter, Maddie, taught me this when she was five years old.

After a day at school in her prep class, she came home and shared all the details of her day with me – imaginative play, building cubby houses, singing and dancing, maths, science experiments and swinging on the monkey bars. Then she added, very matter of factly, 'And I learned about the Power Of Yet today, Mummy.' I asked her what this meant. She told me that just because she can't do something today, doesn't mean she'll never be able to do it. She learned that rather than saying, 'I can't do that', she can say, 'I can't do that, yet' as a way to let herself know that she is still learning.

Wow, she just schooled me in how to build a growth mindset. #THATSMYGIRL

If you remember one thing from *The C Word*, let it be the Power Of Yet. As soon as you place the word YET after a negative statement, you are signalling to your brain that you're not finished growing yet.

- I'm not ready for a committed relationship . . . YET.
- I don't have the skills for my dream job . . . YET.
- I haven't got enough money . . . YET.

IF YOU REMEMBER

one thing from

The C Word,

let it be the

POWER OF YET.

- I'm not fit enough . . . YET.
- I don't like my hair . . . YET.

Can you see how simple this is? This tiny word flicks a switch in your brain and instantly changes the script from 'I can't' to 'I'm learning' and from 'I'm hopeless' to 'I'm hopeful'.

If my Mini-Me can understand and apply this to her life, surely you can apply it to yours?

WHERE TO NEXT?

The *2021 Women's Agenda Ambition Report* was based on a survey of more than 1400 Australian women about what they want from their careers and what they believe would stand in their way.[48]

Next time someone cheekily asks you, 'What do women want?', tell them this:

1. I'm looking to earn more (36 per cent of the surveyed women).

2. I'm looking for a new role (28 per cent).

3. I'm looking to undertake further education (26 per cent).

4. I'm aiming to get promoted (26 per cent).

5. I'm looking to achieve better flexible working options (23 per cent).[49]

In short, we want more. I have no doubt that similar themes would emerge if we asked women what they want in other areas of life too. Relationships, finances, health, friendships, family, travel – we want more!

As women, we have come to know our worth. We no longer calmly accept the lot that is handed to us; we question what is handed to us, then pursue more. Because our collective confidence has developed over the generations, we have built up our self-esteem ('I deserve it') and self-efficacy ('I can do it') and we are no longer in a position to play the submissive maiden. We want more.

But this is a journey and, while we have made inroads, there is still a way to go. The C word remains a barrier to success for many women, and this is why I had no choice BUT to write this book.

The top five reported hurdles in the way of the above ambitions were:

1. lack of confidence in abilities (45 per cent)

2. burnout (39 per cent)

3. caring responsibilities, including children (31 per cent)

4. age discrimination (30 per cent)

5. gender discrimination (25 per cent).[50]

According to the Women's Agenda research, the top two things that women perceive as barriers to success are **lack of confidence and working too hard**. I would suggest that these are two factors that are mostly within your control, and common themes throughout *The C Word*. My hope for you, now that you've come to the end of this book, is that you are now starting to feel that confidence and burnout are things that you can tackle, things that you are now empowered to change.

On the plus-side, the Women's Agenda research revealed one very optimistic fact: women's confidence is improving! When they asked women the same questions back in 2017, 51 per cent identified 'confidence in my abilities' as the top perceived barrier to their success; in 2021, it's down to 45 per cent.[51]

Now, that's progress.

HERE'S TO THE SISTERHOOD

Before I sign off, I have a personal confession to share with you.

We've talked at length about Imposter Syndrome and you'd be excused for thinking that I, as a highly confident woman, might be immune to such experiences. And, until very recently, you'd be right. For many years, I found it a little challenging to write and speak about Imposter Syndrome because I genuinely had no personal experience with it.

Until I wrote this book.

And, no, the irony is not lost on me!

I've worn many hats in my career – psychologist, counsellor, therapist, consultant, coach, mentor, speaker, leader, presenter, facilitator – but until now I've never identified myself as an author. To me, authors were people who got As in English at school (I certainly didn't), studious people, really, really smart and articulate people who spent their lives reading books. Although I enjoy reading, I'd honestly rather watch a good TV series than spend all afternoon immersed in a book.

Even as I write this now, I can't believe I've written a book. This (fear-based belief system) became really clear to me when my publisher asked for my opinion on the cover design. She sent me through an initial idea and I froze – my instinct was to say that I wanted a bigger picture of myself on the cover but my Imposter Syndrome voice popped up and said, 'You're barely even an author, you do not have the right to make demands about your picture on the cover. Accept what you're given.' The idea that I wanted a bigger photo actually made me feel deeply embarrassed, ashamed and falsely entitled. So, I consulted with my power team of supportive and talented women – Kylie and Susie of the Lime Agency – and shared my apprehension. Before I knew it, Kylie had emailed my publisher with a range of alternative suggestions for cover designs, ones that more closely represented my personal brand. The cover you see today came about through my team's deep understanding of me, their recognition that I needed a little extra support and the sensational power of collaboration.

Sometimes, you just need a little help from your friends.

ENDNOTES

1   D. Ropeik, 'The consequences of fear', *EMBO Reports*, 2004, 5, Spec No(Suppl 1), S56–S60.
2   ibid.
3   ibid.
4   A.W. Brooks, 'Get excited: Reappraising pre-performance anxiety as excitement', *Journal of Experimental Psychology: General*, 143, 3 (June 2014), pp. 1144–58.
5   Norman Doidge, *The Brain That Changes Itself: Stories of Personal Triumph from the Frontiers of Brain Science*, Scribe Publications, Melbourne, 2010, p. xvi.
6   Carol Dweck, *Mindset: Changing the Way You Think to Fulfil Your Potential*, Little Brown, London, 2017.
7   Susan David, *Emotional Agility: Get Unstuck, Embrace Change, and Thrive in Work and Life,* Avery Publishing Group, USA, 2016.
8   This statistic comes from a Hewlett Packard internal report.
9   J.A. Nielsen, B.A. Zielinski, M.A. Ferguson, J.E. Lainhart and J.S. Anderson, 'An evaluation of the left-brain vs. right-brain hypothesis with resting state functional connectivity magnetic resonance imaging', *PLOS One*, 8, 8, 2013, e71275.
10 P.M. Lewinsohn, I.H. Gotlib, M. Lewinsohn, J.R. Seeley and N.B. Allen, 'Gender differences in anxiety disorders and anxiety symptoms in adolescents', *Journal of Abnormal Psychology*, 107, 1, 1998, pp. 109–117.
11 beyondblue.org.au/the-facts/anxiety.
12 ibid.
13 beyondblue.org.au/the-facts/anxiety/signs-and-symptoms.
14 S. Watson, 'The unheard female voice', *ASHA Leader*, 24, 2, 2019, pp. 44–53.
15 M. James, 'React vs respond: What's the difference?', *Psychology Today*, 1 September 2016, psychologytoday.com.
16 ibid.
17 Barbara Markway and Celia Ampel, *The Self-Confidence Workbook: A Guide to Overcoming Self-Doubt and Improving Self-Esteem*, Althea Press, 2018.
18 A. Hartmans, P. Leskin and S. Jackson, 'The rise and fall of Elizabeth Holmes', businessinsider.com, 1 September 2021.
19 J. Rampton, '23 amazingly successful introverts throughout history', Inc.com, 20 July 2015.
20 M. Weinberger and P. Leskin, 'The rise and fall of Marissa Mayer', businessinsider. com, 12 February 2020.

21 J.P. Simmons and U. Simonsohn, 'Power posing: P-curving the evidence', *Psychological Science*, forthcoming, quoted in E. Young, '54 study analysis says power posing does affect people's emotions', *The British Psychological Society Research Digest*, 28 March 2018.

22 A.J.C. Cuddy, S.J. Schultz and N.E. Fosse, 'P-curving a more comprehensive body of research on postural feedback reveals clear evidential value for power-posing effects: Reply to Simmons and Simonsohn (2017)', *Psychological Science*, 29, 4, 2018, pp. 656–66.

23 A. Zaccaro, A. Piarulli, M. Laurino, E. Garbella, D. Menicucci, B. Neri and A. Gemignani, 'How breath-control can change your life: A systematic review on psycho-physiological correlates of slow breathing', *Frontiers in Human Neuroscience*, 12, 2018, p. 353.

24 R. McDiarmid, 'The importance of breathing in yoga', yogabhoga.com, March 13, 2015, yogabhoga.com/blog/importance-breathing-yoga.

25 dictionary.com/browse/vapor

26 W. Safire, 'The way we live now: On language – the vapors', *New York Times*, 24 March 2002, nytimes.com.

27 D. Schawbel, 'Brené Brown: How vulnerability can make our lives better', Forbes.com, April 2013.

28 B.L. Fredrickson, 'The broaden-and-build theory of positive emotions', *Philosophical Transactions of the Royal Society of London. Series B, Biological Sciences*, 359, 1449, 2004, pp. 1367–78.

29 B.L. Fredrickson, 'The role of positive emotions in positive psychology. The broaden-and-build theory of positive emotions', *The American Psychologist*, 56, 3, 2001, pp. 218–26.

30 B. Bilanich, 'Self-confidence, optimism and success', *Fast Company*, August 2009, fastcompany.com.

31 K. Ginsburg, 'The 7 Cs: The essential building blocks of resilience', fostering resilience.com/7cs.php.

32 C. Ackerman, '23 amazing health benefits of mindfulness for body and brain', *Positive Psychology*, March 2021, positivepsychology.com.

33 M. Stratton, '6 incredibly successful celebrities who've publicly grappled with burnout', businessinsider.com, October 2019.

34 P. Koutsimani, A. Montgomery, E. Masoura and E. Panagopoulou, 'Burnout and cognitive performance', *International Journal of Environmental Research and Public Health*, 18, 4, 2021, article 2145.

35 International Classification of Diseases, ICD-11 for Mortality and Morbidity Statistics (Version: 05/2021), QD85 Burnout, https://icd.who.int/browse11/l-m/en#/ http://id.who.int/icd/entity/129180281.

36 ibid.

37 thedecisionlab.com/reference-guide/psychology/satisficing.

38 D. Maine, 'World tennis No. 1 Ash Barty calls her stunning decision to retire "scary but exciting"', ESPN.com, 24 March 2022.

39 Richard Wiseman, *The Luck Factor*, Random House, UK, 2004.

40 Intermountain Healthcare, 'Seven ways kindness improves your health', March 2019, intermountainhealthcare.org/blogs/topics/live-well/2019/03/7-ways-kindness-improves-your-health.

41 positivepsychology.com/wp-content/uploads/Gratitude-Letter1.

42 A. Mysoor, 'How women can use monthly periods as a productivity tool', Forbes.com, 10 May 2018.

43 ibid.

44 S. Worso, 'Menstrual cycle mapping', focusboosterapp.com, 8 March 2020, focusboosterapp.com/blog/menstrual-cycle-mapping-how-women-can-improve-their-productivity-and-health-period.

45 A. Mysoor, op. cit.

46 Mary Ann Sieghart, *The Authority Gap*, Penguin, Australia, 2021.

47 William Ury, *The Power of a Positive No*, Random House, USA, 2007.

48 Women's Agenda, 'The 2021 Women's Agenda ambition report', womensagenda.com.au/wp-content/uploads/2021/10/Womens_Ambition-Report_by_Womens_Agenda.pdf

49 Women's Agenda, 'Burnout and confidence are real concerns for women on path to achieving their ambitions', 8 October 2021, womensagenda.com.au/latest/burnout-and-confidence-are-real-concerns-for-women-on-path-to-achieving-their-ambitions.

50 ibid.

51 ibid.

ACKNOWLEDGMENTS

My greatest supporter, challenger and cheerleader is my hubby, Mr Practical, AKA Gareth Brisbane. This man is *My Rock* in every sense of the word – he steps in to take over the home front when I need to work interstate or overseas, he provides me with the sense of stability and security I need to launch all my courageous pursuits. Without him, none of this exists. Gareth and Maddie have given me the most incredible *Home Base*, the most powerful confidence-enabler I've ever experienced. He often jokes that he is the 'wind beneath my wings' and, between you and me, it's no joke. He is comfortable letting me take the spotlight (as long as he can give strategic advice from the wings). Having G walk beside me is my greatest privilege and I couldn't be more grateful. My North Star.

In my professional life, I am so fortunate to be surrounded by a female-powered group of superstars. In Australia, The Lime Agency looks after my career with Kylie Green steering the ship and Susie Pfann managing daily tactics. Kylie is my deal-queen and has the most exquisite black book in the industry. Susie is quite literally my right hand and has saved my flighty ass on a number of occasions (yep, I'm distracted by shiny things!). In the UK, Arlington Talent has my back and I'm so excited to begin my next chapter in London with Hilary Murray and Tatty Black. I'm ever grateful to my talented media lawyer, Yasmin Naghavi, for her keen eye and tenacity. I have excellent working relationships with the fabulous production teams at Endemol Shine Australia and CPL Productions in London, as well as the broader teams at both Channel Nine and Channel Four.

And, of course, this book would be nothing but a pile of messy notes if not for the genius team at Murdoch Books. My publisher, Jane Morrow, has shown such flexibility and elegance in the face of my ever-evolving deadlines. Justin Wolfers, as editorial manager, found a way to deliver tricky feedback in a warm and supportive manner, while keeping me motivated. And then there is Alexandra Payne, my editor. As a first-time writer (with emerging Imposter Syndrome), I was apprehensive about having all the fine details of my book picked apart by an editor – but Alex was divine! So gentle, so smart, so articulate and, importantly, she picked up *my voice* immediately and we worked as a seamless team throughout. Thank you all.